P9-DYE-083

# The Next Wave

For Cobi and Izzi, who love the ocean



www.hmhco.com

Book design by Greta Sibley and Rebecca Bond.
The text of this book is set in Garamond.

*Library of Congress Cataloging-in-Publication Data*
Rusch, Elizabeth.
The next wave : the quest to harness the power of the oceans / by Elizabeth Rusch.
pages cm — (Scientists in the field)
Includes bibliographical references and index.
ISBN 978-0-544-09999-9
1. Ocean energy resources—Juvenile literature. 2. Tidal power—Juvenile literature. 3. Renewable energy sources—Juvenile literature. I. Title.
TC147.R87 2014
621.31'2134—dc23
2013050150
Printed in Singapore
TWP 10 9 8 7 6 5 4 3 2 1
4500473788

Photo credits: Eon Amon/OSU/courtesy of Annette von Jouanne: 55 (main). Aquamarine Power: 35 (left). Jeffrey Basinger: 5 (top right), 39 (right), 46, 50, 51, 52 (main), 53 (bottom right), 58 (main), 59 (main), 60, 61 (main), 62, 63 (main). Jeffrey Basinger/Courtesy of University Marketing, Oregon State University: 4 (top right), 27. Cheryl Casey/Shutterstock: 66 (left), 67 (right). Columbia Power Technologies, Inc.: 56. Delos-Reyes family: 4 (bottom, far right), 14 (main). DigitalVision/Getty Images: 7, 13, 23, 31, 39, 47, 55, 65 (all digitally altered light bulbs). EPA Ocean Survey Vessel Bold/courtesy of Gergory McMurray: 37. Erin Fitzpatrick-Bjorn: 1, 2, 7 (main), 10–11, 17 (right), 18, 30, 38, 39 (left), 40, 42 (right), 43 (right), 64, 70, 71. Getty Images: 4 (top left), 8, 9. Jenny Goldstick: 15, 17, 25, 33, 49 (graphics). Erica Harris, Oregon State University: 6. Cheryl Hatch: 23, 24, 26 (right). Image Source/Getty Images: 25, 58 (background). Gregg Keene: 18 (background). M3 Wave/Marty Manning: 42 (left). M3 Wave/Mike Morrow: 5 (top left), 20, 21 (left), 41, 43 (left), 44, 45. Morrow family: 4 (bottom, far left), 13. NASA: 5 (bottom right), 73. Rachel Newborn: 11 (map). Nito/Shutterstock: 8, 9, 52 (background). Ocean Power Technologies, Inc.: 65, 66 (right), 67 (left), 68, 69. Oceanlinx Ltd.: 35 (right). Oregon State University College of Engineering: 19, 54. Oregon State University/Pat Knight/Oregon Sea Grant: 47, 49 (top left, bottom right), 53 (top right), 57. Pelamis Wave Power: 34 (left). Photodisc/Getty Images: 3, 25, 31 and 13, 39, 43 (screened back images). Randy L. Rasmussen/the Oregonian: 5 (bottom left), 53 (top left). Radu Razvan/Shutterstock: 23, 36, 65 (screened back images). Brian Smale: 22, 31. Gail Sumida/courtesy of Annette von Jouanne: 29. Giuseppe Tiberini/Flickr/GettyImages: 11, 25, 28, 34, 35, 48 (sidebar outlines). Vladgrin/Fotolia: 14, 19, 20, 45, 59, 61, 63 (all digitally altered graphics). Annette von Jouanne: 26 (left), 32, 48, 72. Water World, Joann V. Cortez, Colorado: 16. Wave Dragon: 34 (right). Alla Weinstein: 4 (bottom right), 36.

# The Next Wave

## THE QUEST TO HARNESS THE POWER OF THE OCEANS

*by* **Elizabeth Rusch**

Houghton Mifflin Harcourt
Boston New York

# CONTENTS

1 The Power of Waves 7

2 The Mikes 13

3 Building Buoys 23

4 Steel in the Water 31

5 Ducking the Waves 39

7 Big Power from Big Seas 55

6 Testing, Testing 47

8 Saved by Waves? 65

Wave Words 74

A Big Wave of Thanks 74

Notes 74

Sources 76

Read—and Surf—More 78

Index 79

Waves pound the shore between Depot Bay and Boiler Bay on the Oregon coast

# 1

# The Power of Waves

Never turn your back on the ocean. That's a good rule to live by when you're near the sea. If you don't follow it, you could be knocked over, get pummeled—or even perish.

The moving, swelling, surging movement of water in the ocean holds astonishing force. If you've ever played in the waves at the beach, you've experienced a hint of their power as the foamy water rushing in and out tugs at your ankles. If you venture deeper, the waves can lift you up, flip you over, and knock you down.

Waves carve rock and sculpt cliffs. Waves pound pebbles and shells into smithereens, crushing them into tiny bits that we call sand. A wave that is just a foot and a half high can topple a wall built to withstand hurricane-force winds. And that power is just as fierce out in the open ocean.

A girl plays in the waves in Cinnamon Bay in the U.S. Virgin Islands.

In 2001, one of the strongest cruise ships in the world, called the *Caledonian Star,* received a warning of gale-force winds on the way. The ship was built to withstand the thick ice and harsh seas of the Antarctic, so no one was worried, at first.

The storm hit, surrounding the boat with churning, turbulent water. Waves thirty feet (9 meters) high rose up, with steep, frothing, spraying crests and deep, dark troughs. Peaks reached so high that they couldn't support their own weight, and massive walls of water crashed down. But the ship weathered the waves well.

Then-first officer Göran Persson spotted something off in the distance—a huge wave, twice as big as the rest. "It was just like a mountain, a wall of water coming against us," Göran says. "It wasn't a sloping wave; it was a vertical wall of solid green water."

As the wave approached, a monstrous trough opened up before the ship, which tipped and went into a free fall. Tourists onboard fell forward, toward the bulk-

A view of a wave from a ship in Drakes Passage in the South Atlantic, one of the roughest bodies of sea in the world.

heads. Then the wave slammed into the *Caledonian Star,* burying its bow in a wall of water nearly a hundred feet (30 meters) tall—as high as a ten-story building. "The whole bridge was like an explosion and I was washed . . . over to the other side," Göran recalls. "Me and the helmsman, we were lying on top of each other underwater fighting books and cushions and [electrical] shorts." The wave completely destroyed the ship's radars, compasses, and sonar, and the crew struggled to control the ship in the harrowing seas. "[It] went through your mind that this, this might be it, we might not make it," Göran says.

But with the engines still working, the crew was able to keep the ship faced into the waves to weather the storm. Eventually they boarded up the busted windows and limped back to port. They were lucky to survive; many are not so fortunate.

Around the globe, thousands of vessels have been dashed against rocks and sunk. And it's not much safer in the middle of the ocean, where massive heaving swells

An oil tanker ship churns up a huge wave in rough seas.

can capsize and smash ships. Every year, on average, more than two dozen large ships disappear. Add smaller boats and the number is much higher.

Throughout human history, people have dreamed of putting some of the frightening, incredible power of ocean waves to good use. Long ago, sailors devised one clever method. They deliberately turned their backs on waves, planning their routes to travel with a "following sea." Ocean swells pushing boats can speed a journey for thousands of miles. Closer to shore, ancient Hawaiians carved long boards out of trees so they could catch and ride waves.

Today, a small group of scientists is searching for ways to harness the awesome power of the ocean. These pioneers are inventing machines to transform the potent pulsing movement of waves into electricity to light our homes and power our lives.

We are in desperate need of a new, clean, renewable energy source. Coal, oil, and natural gas currently provide more than 80 percent of our nation's energy demands. In addition to polluting the air we breathe, burning these fossil fuels pumps huge amounts of carbon dioxide ($CO_2$) into the atmosphere, where it traps heat, gradually and dangerously warming the planet.

Almost all (97 percent) of climate scientists agree that human activities, mostly the burning of fossil fuels, are heating up the earth. Average global temperatures have risen 1.33 degrees Fahrenheit (17 degrees Celsius) since 1880, with a cascade of effects. Average global sea levels have risen almost seven inches (17 centimeters) in the past century. Glaciers are retreating almost everywhere, and Arctic sea ice is melting almost 11 percent every decade. Heat waves, heavy precipitation, and other extreme weather events are becoming more and more frequent.

Waves offer an exciting clean, renewable energy option. Oceans have been called the earth's biggest batteries. That's because they cover almost three-quarters of the earth's surface and store enormous amounts of energy. Wave energy could provide as much as *a third* of the electricity used in the United States. That's the equivalent of the energy provided by more than 93 billion gallons of oil—more than twice the power produced by all U.S. hydroelectric dams, solar power, and wind power projects combined—and enough to power *every home* in the nation.

But first, wave energy engineers have a mighty obstacle to overcome—the sea. Inventors have been struggling for decades to create devices capable of surviving the punishing force of our powerful oceans. "To be successful, an ocean-energy device needs to do two things," says Justin Klure, a consultant who has worked with a number of ocean-energy pioneers. "It must harness the power of the waves and convert it into electricity, of course. But it also has to survive. To extract the power of a wave, you need direct contact with the wave. But you can't let the waves break your machine. It's hard to overstate how difficult it really is to achieve that balance."

Despite these overwhelming challenges, the work of these ocean energy pioneers is finally reaching a crest, with an array of amazing machines proving their worth in the water. Nowhere is this more evident than in the Pacific Northwest, where some of the biggest, most energetic waves batter a long stretch of coastline almost year-round. Engineers there have developed ingenious ways to transform the fierce power of those waves into electricity to energize our lives. This is their story.

A surfer catches a wave off the Oregon coast.

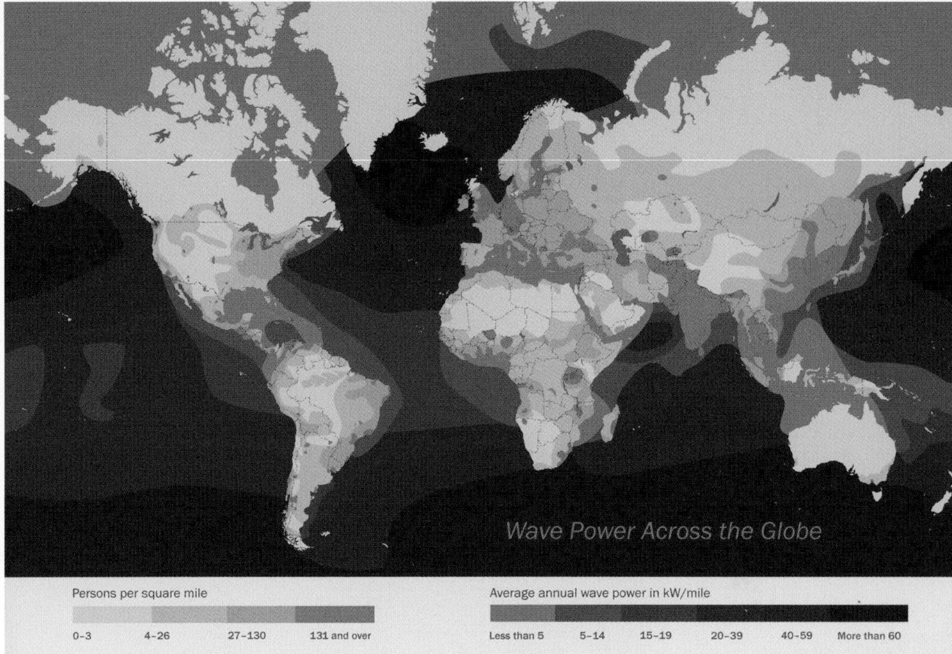


## POWER NEAR THE PEOPLE

A great deal of energy generated around the world is lost from resistance in wires when transported long distances. One of the benefits of ocean energy is that the electricity can be generated—and used—near where people live. More than half the U.S. population lives near the coast and more than half the world's population lives within 125 miles (200 kilometers) of the ocean. Eight of the ten biggest cities are on the coast. This map shows population density (darker means more densely populated) and the areas with the best wave energy potential (deep purple colors). See how close many people are to the biggest, most powerful waves?

Weatherford Hall at Oregon State University in Corvallis, Oregon

# 2

# The Mikes

Mike Morrow and Mike Delos-Reyes grew up together near Salem, Oregon. They played at the park, rode bikes, and made forts. But Mike Morrow was an only child. "At the end of the day, I'd find myself alone in my room, taking things apart," he says.

Mike Morrow was a whiz at reverse engineering, even though he didn't know that's what his favorite activity was called. With a screwdriver, he could open up anything electronic—clocks, radios, even calculators. With a pair of needle-nose pliers in one hand, he'd gently grab one of the tiny parts. With a soldering iron in the other hand, he'd melt the metal that was holding the part in place and pull it clear off. "I had a huge collection of these tiny colorful components all separated into compartments," he says. "For the longest time I didn't even know what they

LEFT: Mike Morrow measures wind speed with an anemometer he made using plastic egg halves glued to an egg beater.
RIGHT: Mike Morrow prepares to view a solar eclipse.
FAR RIGHT: Mike Morrow wins first place with a science fair project on the chemical composition of water.

were. But I knew they were important and totally cool and I figured that someday, somehow, I could recombine them into various new inventions."

When he was in elementary school, Mike got his hands on two broken calculators and had an idea. What if he could crosswire the calculators and run a cable between them? Maybe he and his friend Mike Delos-Reyes could send messages back and forth to each other in numerical code. "I found out I was better at taking things apart than putting them back together," he says with a laugh.

His friend Mike Delos-Reyes was the perfect complement, though—he had a real knack for building things. He built a guitar out of a badminton racket, welded himself a scooter, and tinkered on cars and bikes with his dad. Together, the Mikes helped start McNary High School's Science Club.

Their senior class voted Mike Morrow Most Likely to Become a Mad Scientist. "I wanted to invent something cool someday," he says. "But I didn't know what."

When Mike Morrow was seventeen years old, he and his dad went to Water World in Denver. Mike was playing in the wave pool when he noticed a handle near the bottom. "I thought it would be fun to see if I could hold on underwater while the wave passed over, to see what that felt like," he says. So he sucked in his breath, dunked under, and held on tight. "As the wave moved over, my ears popped," he says. "It happened every time." Mike

Mike Delos-Reyes, age seventeen, works on a collage.

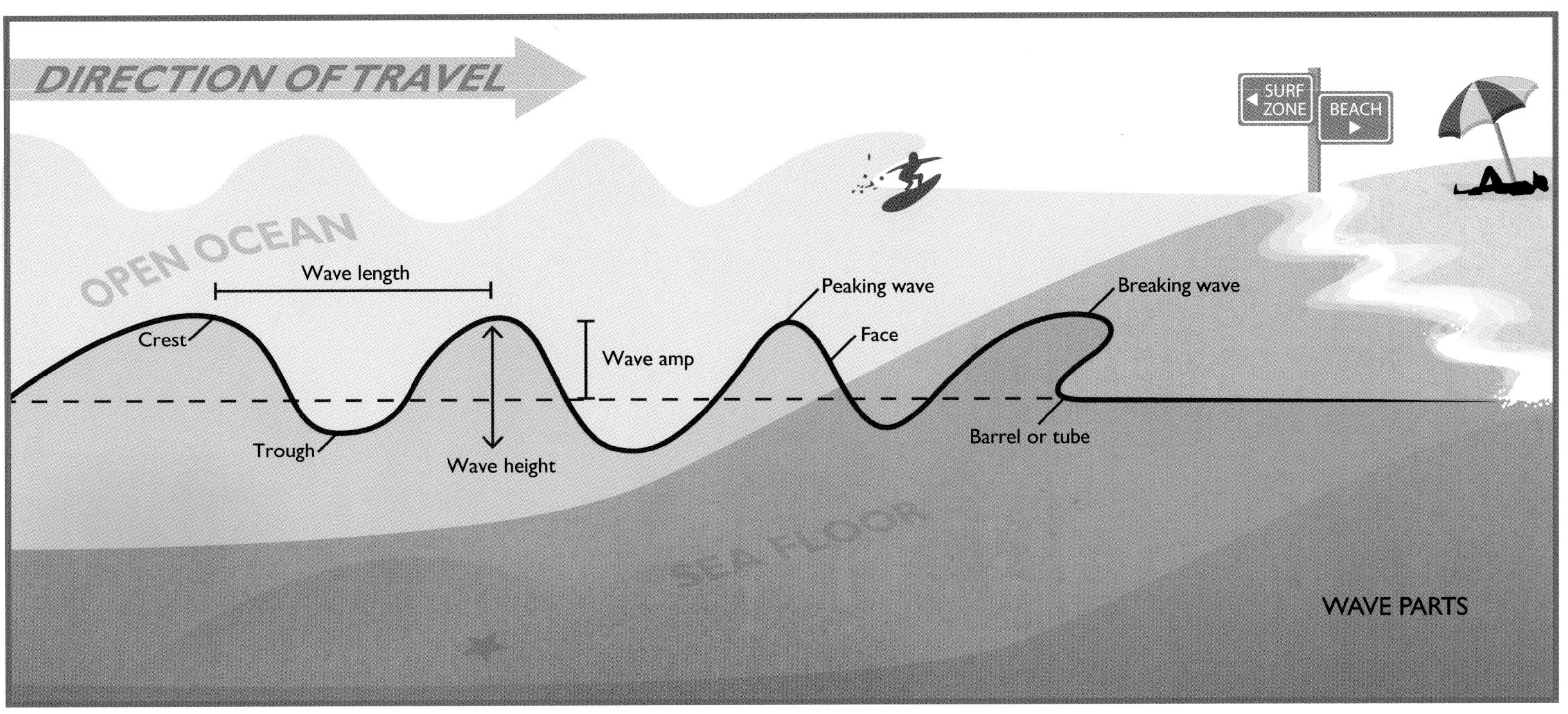


## WHAT ARE WAVES?

As the sun warms the earth, uneven heating causes winds that blow across the ocean. Friction between the moving air and the water beneath it forms ripples on the surface. The more powerful the wind, the longer it blows, and the greater the distance it blows, the bigger the ripples grow. Ripples merge together into waves. After about a hundred miles, disorganized, chaotic seas transform into an organized swell. A swell can keep its speed—and power—for hundreds, even thousands of miles.

The height and shape of waves constantly change as they move across the ocean. Imagine two waves traveling in the same direction but at different speeds. When the crest of one wave lines up with the trough of another, they can virtually cancel each other out. But when the crest of one wave overtakes another, a massive wave can rise up.

knew from scuba diving that you have to pop your ears as you descend because deeper water has higher pressure. *Waves cause pressure changes,* he thought. *Interesting.*

Mike didn't think of it again until he was a senior in college at Oregon State University studying mechanical engineering alongside Mike Delos-Reyes. To graduate, students were required to complete a senior project. Mike and Mike were given a list of possible projects sponsored by companies such as Hewlett-Packard and Nike. But the Mikes didn't want to do a project someone else had created; they wanted to come up with something on their own.

"That's not really the way we do this," the administration told the students. If they wanted to try, they'd have to design a project, define the scope, recruit an advisor, and track down their own materials.

The wave pool at Water World in Denver, where Mike Morrow noticed that waves change the pressure underwater.

The Mikes found an empty classroom with a large chalkboard and started brainstorming. They filled the board with ideas, but none seemed quite right. Then Mike Morrow remembered what happened at the wave park. He told his friend about how his ears popped when waves passed over him.

"Waves cause temporary pressure changes," he said. "There's got to be a way to use that."

"Maybe we could make electricity from the waves," Mike Delos-Reyes said. "That would be cool."

They discussed whether the pressure from the waves could somehow spin a turbine, like wind spins a pinwheel. They got an idea. Maybe high pressure under a wave could compress an underwater air bag on the ocean floor, creating wind in a tube that could spin a turbine, generating electricity. They sketched out a model on the chalkboard. The model had two air bags, one on either side of the turbine. As the wave moved over the first air bag, it would compress it, sending air through the turbine and into the second air bag. And when the wave reached the second air bag, it would compress that one, sending the air back through the turbine and back to the first bag. It would be like a breathing cycle, with the air moving back and forth.

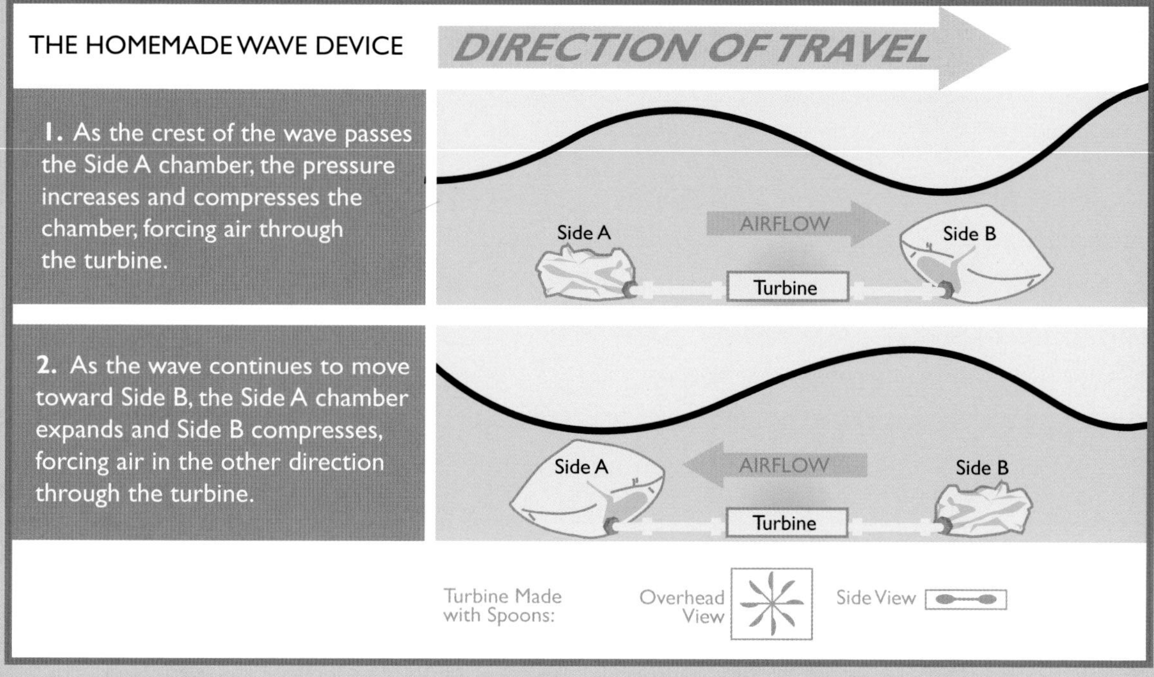


The idea made sense to the Mikes, but they were mechanical engineers and knew very little about ocean engineering. So they pitched it to OSU's only ocean engineering professor, Robert Hudspeth.

"Hmmm," he said. "That could work." The Mikes convinced him to become their project advisor.

This was in 1991, before computer modeling and simulation programs were available to most students. "So the only way we could test if our device would work was to build it," Mike Morrow says.

The Mikes began searching for components. They would need two waterproof flexible bags with a hard opening to attach to the wind pipes. Mike Morrow was in the cafeteria pondering the problem when he saw a worker open up a milk dispenser. He unfastened a big, almost-empty plastic bag and replaced it with one full of milk.

Mike walked up to him. "What do you do with the empty bag?"

The worker looked surprised. "Throw it away."

"Can I have it?" Mike asked.

The worker shrugged and handed him the bag.

"I need another one," Mike said. "Where do you throw them out?"

The worker pointed to the dumpster out back.

Mike climbed in. After digging around among the rotting food scraps, greasy napkins, and sour packaging, he found another bag. But it must have been in there a while. The milk residue inside had turned rancid.

"It was just what we needed," Mike says. "I plugged my nose as I washed it out."

The young inventors wanted something to hold the buoyant bags in place. Water would have to be able to move through whatever held the bags. Ideally, they'd be able to watch how the bags performed inside. The Mikes spotted some plastic milk crates behind a grocery store and snagged them. A visit to the hardware store took care of PVC pipes for the wind tunnels.

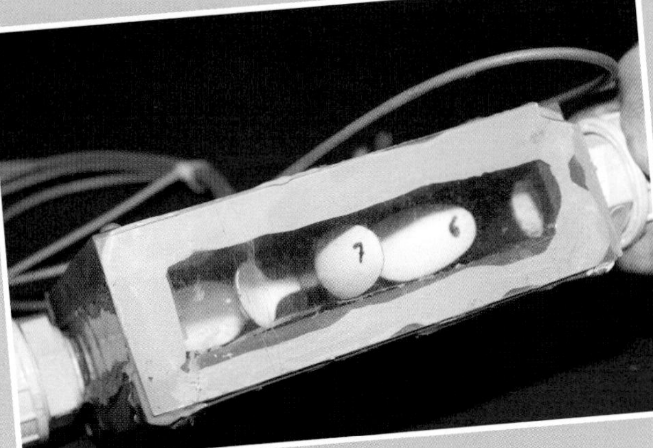

The Mikes' bidirectional turbine made with plastic fast food spoons.

But they still needed an air turbine to place in between the air bags. To make the most of momentum, the turbine would need to continue spinning in one direction even as the air switched directions. The students hit the library to search engineering journals and patents for a bidirectional turbine. They found plans for one that might work, but it looked too complex. So they tried to make one on their own.

"For the turbine blades, I think we need something cupped and curved," Mike Morrow said.

"Maybe I could make them," Mike Delos-Reyes offered.

"What about spoons?" Mike asked.

"We need them to be really light. How about plastic spoons?"

They grinned at each other and raided a nearby fast food restaurant. Mike Delos-Reyes attached the spoons in an array around a hub, like the petals on a flower.

The Mikes started putting the pieces together. They had very different ideas about how to do things and both were opinionated. When they disagreed on an idea, they bet a dollar on it and tried it. "Turns out that's a pretty effective rapid development tool," Mike Morrow says. Instead of wasting time debating good and bad ideas, they tested all the ideas that either one thought was promising.

Before long, they had a contraption to try with their hands. Squeezing one inflated bag sent air though the pipes to the turbine, spinning the plastic spoons, generating electricity, and inflating the other bag. Squeezing the other bag kept the spoons spinning and the turbine generating electricity.

But would swells of water moving over the bags do the same thing? To find out, they needed to test their invention in waves. Putting their device on the bottom of the real ocean was out. Their flimsy contraption would likely be smashed to bits. Plus it was too cold and too dangerous. They couldn't breathe without expensive scuba gear, and moving sand would cloud the water, making it hard to see anything.

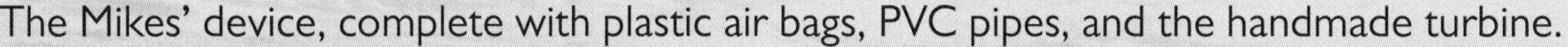

The Mikes' device, complete with plastic air bags, PVC pipes, and the handmade turbine.

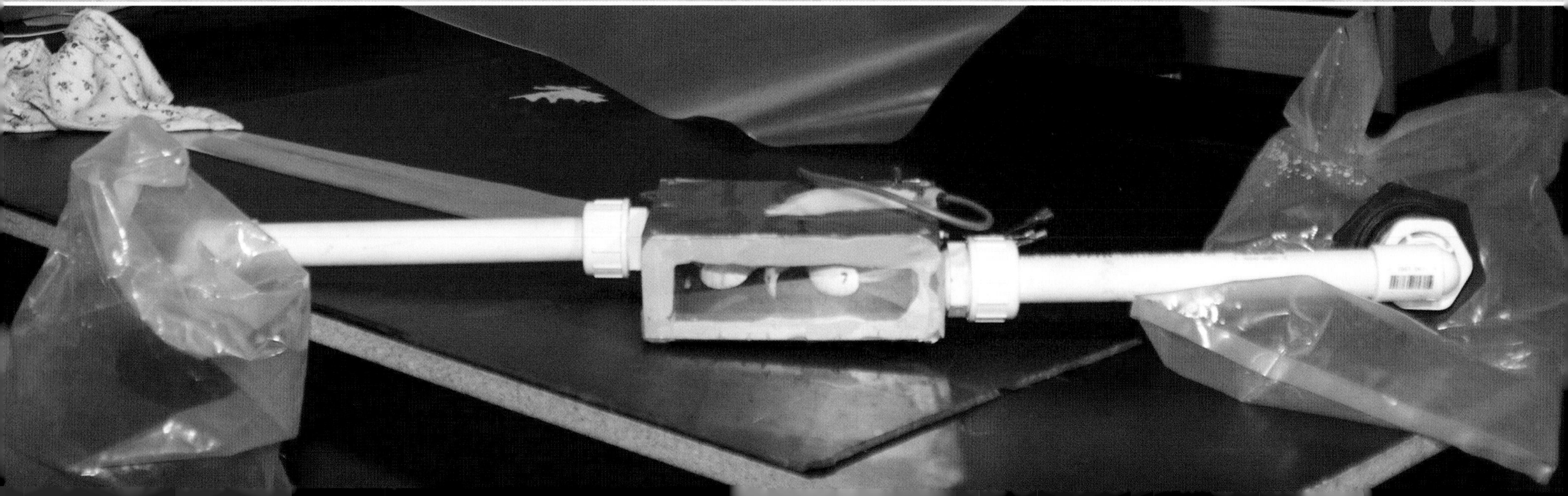

The Mikes visited the O. H. Hinsdale Wave Research Laboratory, a center for coastal engineering research at Oregon State University. The lab's 342-foot wave flume, where you could dial up different-size waves, looked perfect. But then they found out the cost: $3,000 a day.

"Do you offer a student discount?" Mike Morrow asked.

The answer was no.

Back in Graf Hall, one of the engineering buildings, the Mikes had noticed a broken wave tank in a pile of junk, with more junk heaped inside. It looked like a forty-foot-long (12-meter) bathtub with Plexiglas sides. The waterproof seals seemed to still be intact. Maybe it could still hold water. Mike Delos-Reyes examined the wave generating mechanism, a big paddle that shoved the water to make waves. He thought he might be able to get it working.

Late one night, after the janitor had done his rounds, the Mikes snuck into the hall. They cleared away the junk, checked for leaks, and ran a hose from a nearby sink to the tank. The long tank would take hours to fill. In the meantime, Mike Delos-Reyes fixed the tank's wave generating paddle and figured out how to dial up waves of different sizes.

The 342-foot wave flume at OSU's O. H. Hinsdale Wave Research Laboratory.

Mike Morrow (left) and Mike Delos-Reyes (right) try to get their device working in the small wave tank in Graf Hall.

Finally, the tank was full and they were ready to roll. They submerged their contraption, pushed it to the bottom of the tank, and held it down with steel weights. Using a bike pump, they inflated one of the bags. Then they programmed in the first wave.

The paddle moved and a swell of water glided toward the invention. The wave moved over the first air bag.

Nothing happened.

It didn't work.

The Mikes peered in the Plexiglas window as wave after wave rolled over their invention. The inflated bag jiggled around a little but didn't deflate.

Then the Mikes noticed that the inflated bag wasn't lying flat—it had floated up to a vertical position.

"Look, the bag is pinching off the opening . . ." one Mike said.

". . . cutting off the air flow," the other Mike finished.

They crafted a quick-and-dirty solution. They cut off two small sections of an old rubber hose they found in a nearby pile of lab junk, one for each bag. To keep the bag from pinching shut, they stuck one end of the hose into the air pipe and the other end deep into the bag. The hose kept the plastic from folding up and covering the opening.

The Mikes submerged the contraption again, inflated the bag, and watched as a swell glided from the paddle toward the invention. The wave moved over the first air bag. The water pressure compressed the air bag, pushing air, which spun the spoons and the turbine. The wave continued, compressing the second bag and continuing the spin of the turbine.

The Mikes whistled and cheered: "It works! It really works!"

During that night and the next, the Mikes tried the device with different wave heights and lengths. Their device performed well in a wide variety of waves. They wrote up their report, presented it, and passed with flying colors. The pair took home medals in regional, national, and international engineering competitions. Then they graduated, packed the device in a cardboard crate, and stashed it in Mike Morrow's mom's attic.

The Mikes didn't open the crate again for two decades.

The Mikes' device generating electricity in 1991.

Annette von Jouanne, an Oregon State University professor, on a bluff overlooking the Pacific Ocean.

3

# Building Buoys

A few years after the Mikes graduated, Annette von Jouanne joined Oregon State University, but not as a student, as a professor. Like the Mikes, Annette spent many childhood hours tinkering with things—clocks, computers, even her family's television. "I would wait until I knew my parents were going to be gone for a long enough amount of time that I could get something apart and back together again," Annette admits with a smile.

But for Annette, engineering was all in the family. She had two older brothers studying to be engineers. When they came home from college they told her about their projects in school and showed her their textbooks. "It firmed up for me that, yes, this is what I want to do," she says.

Annette even knew what kind of engineer she wanted to be: an electrical engineer. "From a very young age, I was always interested in energy—how electricity is

Swimming is still all in the family for Annette von Jouanne. She is pictured here underwater with her husband, Alex Yokochi, a three-time Olympic swimmer, and her two daughters, Sydney and Naiya. She also has a son, Luke, born after this picture was taken.

Annette von Jouanne finishes a surfing session on the Oregon coast.

generated, power systems, components, everything," she says. So she couldn't wait to start as assistant professor of electrical engineering at Oregon State, where she would be able to work in the highest-power energy-systems lab in the country. But what, exactly, would she work on there?

Making the world a better place was at the top of her list. Annette was concerned about our heavy use of nonrenewable resources, how much we burned fossil fuels for energy, and all the pollution they made. She wanted to work on clean, fuel-free energy—renewable energy. "We're living on this amazing planet and I wanted to help people, help future generations have a positive energy future," she says. But she wasn't sure exactly how.

Annette grew up in a family of swimmers. She and her two brothers and sister all raced on swim teams. Sometimes Annette swam three times a day—she always carried a bathing suit in her backpack so she could take a dip in the pool or in one of the lakes and rivers near Seattle whenever an opportunity arose.

The ocean simply mesmerized Annette. "I loved just watching wave after wave of heaving swells roll in," she says, "or building sandcastles on the beach and then watching waves come in and destroy them. There's just this amazing energy that you can see with your own eyes."

Annette felt the power of the waves, too, whenever she boogie-boarded or bodysurfed in the ocean. One day, Annette went bodysurfing. As the waves lifted her from the sand and propelled her headfirst toward the shore, she found herself thinking about renewable energy sources like solar and wind. The sun dipping below the horizon made her think about all the solar panels that would have no more solar energy hitting them. The lack of wind made her think about all the wind turbines that were slowing and stopping. And still, the waves just kept coming.

"As the sun set, it hit me: I could ride waves all day and even all night, all year long," she says. "Wave power is always there. It never stops. I began thinking that there's got to be a way to harness this energy."

Annette had been pummeled by big waves at the beach many times, so she knew that waves could also be incredibly destructive. There would be other challenges, too. Would a wave-energy device be able to endure tangling seaweed, floating logs, and animals of the sea or sky? Could she create a way to generate enough electricity to make a real difference?

Annette wanted to try the simplest, most direct way to convert the up-and-down motion of waves into electrical

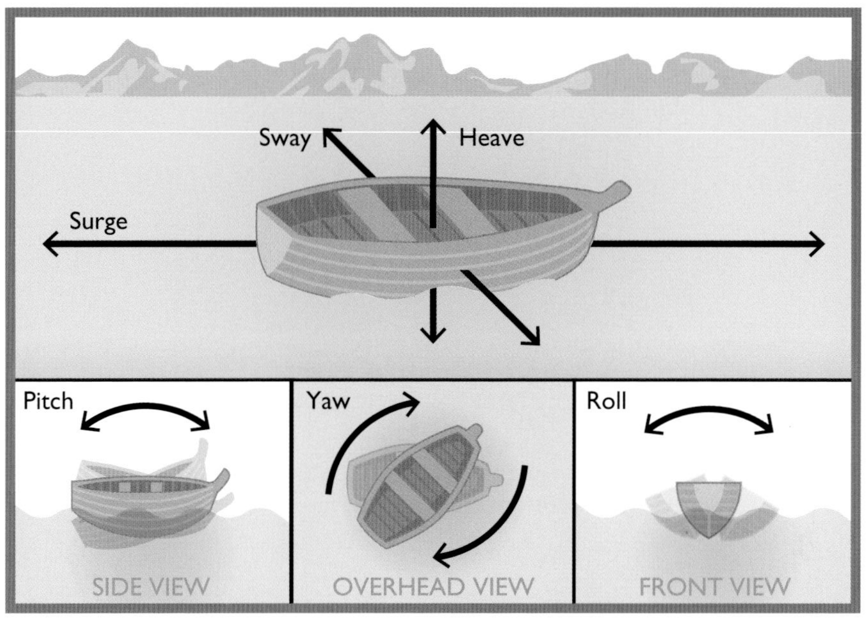


## RIDING THE WAVES

Something floating in the ocean with waves passing under it can bob up and down (heave), move front and back (surge), and slide side to side (sway). Depending on how an object is moored, it may also rotate around its central axis.

A wave may cause an energy device to . . .

- pitch, or teeter like a seesaw, the front plowing down while the back sticks up and vice versa
- yaw, or rotate toward the left or the right
- roll, or tip toward the left or the right

Wave energy inventors must decide which of these movements to harness to make electricity—and which to just make sure the device can survive.

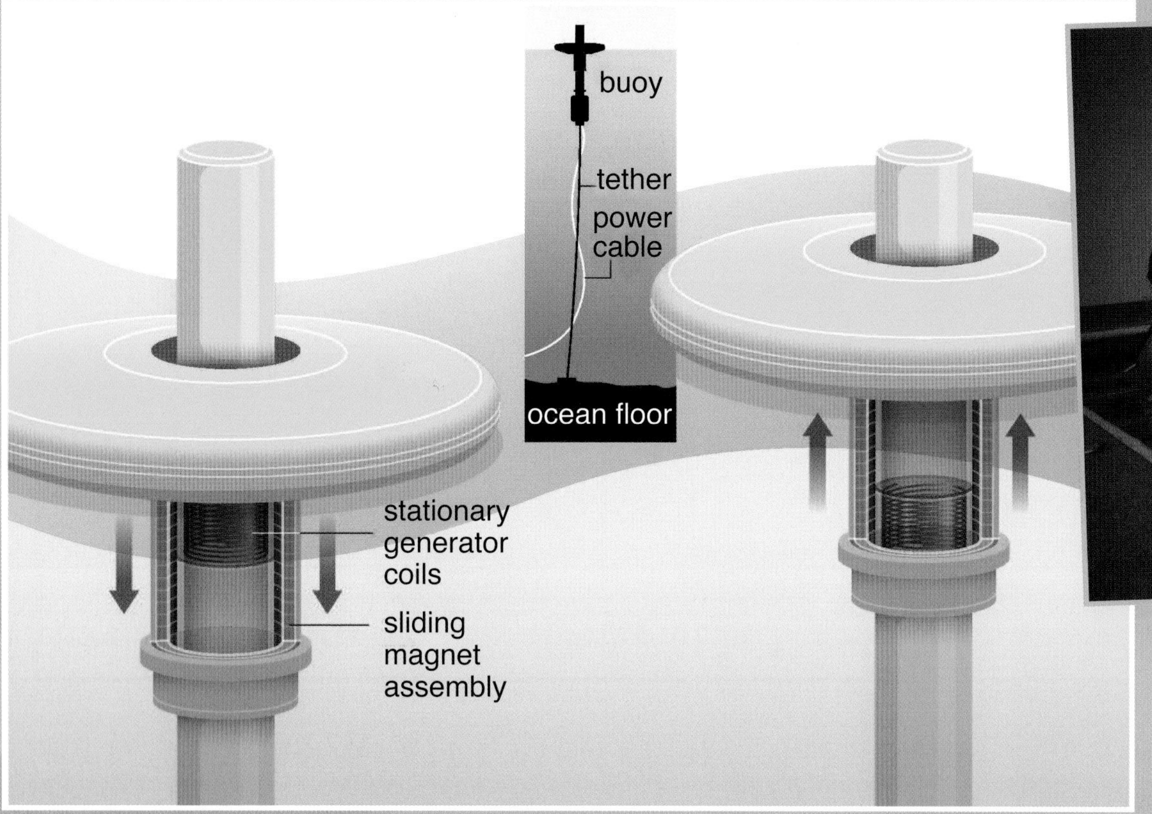


Annette von Jouanne's group teamed up with Columbia Power Technologies on this linear generator prototype buoy design. Magnets moving with the buoy slide past coils inducing electricity.

Annette von Jouanne in her family's dual swim flume, where she tested wave buoy prototypes.

energy. She and her colleagues at OSU thought a bobbing buoy with magnets was a good approach to investigate. For five years, Annette wrote proposals to the U.S. Department of Energy asking for money to develop their ideas. For five years, she didn't get a penny. "That door just kept closing, closing, closing," she recalls. Finally, she landed her first funding from the National Science Foundation. It wasn't much, but it was enough for them to start building and testing small prototypes.

Right away, Annette and her colleagues involved students in the projects. "They immediately developed a passion for wave energy," she says, coming up with creative designs, debating options, and assembling the components. "We had buoy components all over the lab," she says, "and we spent more than a thousand hours putting various buoys together."

Their first prototypes had two main parts—coils of copper wire and magnets. For example, some prototypes had the coils of copper wire inside a thick, strong pole, called a spar, that would be located near the surface of the water and anchored to the sea floor so it wouldn't move. The second part was a float like a donut around the first part that would float freely up and down with the waves. This bobbing float had hundreds of magnets. As the magnets moved with the waves, the magnetic field moved along the coils of copper wire. This motion would induce voltages and current in the wire—generating electricity.

Annette von Jouanne, a professor in the College of Engineering at Oregon State University, holds her breath underwater while adjusting ballast (weights) on a wave-energy device for testing in a pool.

"As electrical engineers, we were really focused on the technology to generate electricity," she says. "We weren't so sure about the buoy structure." So she had to test whether the buoys were waterproof and buoyant. She plunked one into her family's swim flume, a small pool that circulates water to allow for swimming in place. Annette was relieved that the buoy was watertight—and it floated.

The next step was to test the device's stability in heaving water. Annette got in touch with the nearby Splash! wave park.

"Do you rent out your pool?" she asked.

"For how many people?" they asked, thinking she was hosting a birthday party.

"Not many people, but one wave energy buoy," she answered.

The staff had read about her in the local paper, so they let her use the wave park for free before regular pool hours. Annette and her students hauled the device to the pool, where the familiar smell of chlorine hung in the air. They realized they couldn't bolt the steel anchor plate of the device to the pool bottom. So they improvised. Annette and her students welded knee-high posts onto the steel plate before positioning it on the pool floor with the posts sticking up. They borrowed ten 45-pound weights from an OSU exercise room, and Annette carefully walked the weights into the tepid water one by one. As she moved deeper and deeper, the weights held her underwater, as if she were wearing cement shoes. She held her breath as she positioned the weights onto the posts, being vigilant not to spring up too quickly under the buoy and hit her head.

With the device "anchored" to the bottom and floating on the surface, they turned on the waves. The waves rose and the device went up and down without sinking.

They were ready to test the prototype's stability and electricity generation in much bigger waves—at OSU's O. H. Hinsdale Wave Research Lab, in the big wave flume the Mikes couldn't afford when they were students there.

## WORKING WITH WATTS

Electrical power is measured in watts. Electrical bills for most American homes are in kilowatt-hours. A typical household has an average power consumption of roughly 1 kilowatt, or 1,000 watts, with most of the energy going to heating and running appliances.

The wattage of most appliances is usually stamped somewhere on the device. These are some typical wattages:

- iPod: 1 watt
- Clock radio: 10 watts
- Incandescent light bulb: 60 watts
- Flat-screen television: 120 watts
- Computer monitor: 150 watts
- Microwave: 750–1,100 watts
- Hair dryer: 1,200–1,875 watts
- Dishwasher: 1,200–2,400 watts

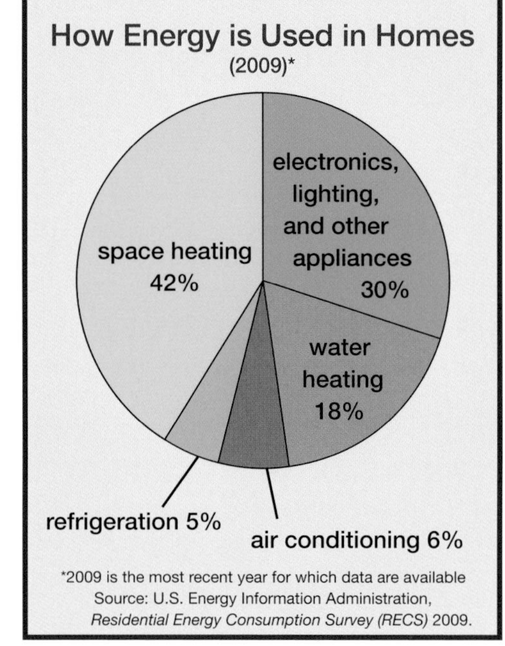


Wave-energy devices are also given wattage ratings, based on the maximum power they are expected to generate. A 40-kilowatt device can generate 40 kilowatts of electricity, which can power a thousand 40-watt light bulbs—or forty typical American households. Wave energy engineers are striving to develop bigger devices or arrays of devices powerful enough to generate megawatts of electricity. A megawatt equals 1,000 kilowatts, so a wave-energy device generating 5 megawatts could power up to five thousand homes.

The wave research lab is dozens of miles inland from the ocean, but still has a sign that warns ENTERING TSUNAMI HAZARD ZONE. Inside the massive tin shed, the Large Wave Flume looks like a giant concrete aqueduct, longer than a football field. At one end, a wave maker pushes water to form waves that roll from one end of the flume to the other.

Annette and her students plopped the device in the water and secured it to the bottom. They started small, with two-, three-, and four-foot waves. The device looked lopsided, and it lurched and wobbled and bobbed in the waves. Then they cranked the waves up to five feet (1.5 meters), the biggest the buoy had faced. When the first wave hit, the device teetered to one side and tipped over.

"In the preliminary stages of development, there are going to be some failures," Annette says. "There are going to be years of trials and successes and failures as we try to move this technology forward."

The team figured out that they had a ballast problem. That meant they had to find a better way to distribute the weight in the device so it would be more stable in bigger waves. "But we're electrical engineers, and we really needed more help from ocean engineers," she says. "To get them we needed more funding, and to get more funding we needed to show some success."

So, Annette and her team kept at it, redesigning, rebuilding, and retesting in the waves. Finally, Annette brought a revised model of the original to the flume. "We were excited, just hoping that all the components would operate properly," she says. "We knew a lot of different parts had to work together and that if one piece didn't work, the whole thing wouldn't work." They set up the buoy and a small group, including her students, gathered. When a five-foot (1.5-meter) wave hit, the device lifted with the wave.

A 40-watt light bulb lit up.

The engineers cheered.

Annette von Jouanne stands near the large wave flume at OSU's O. H. Hinsdale Wave Research Laboratory, where she tested her wave device prototypes.

Powerful waves roll in along the Pacific Northwest coast.

# 4

# Steel in the Water

It's one thing to test a wave-energy device in a wave flume on dry land. It's another thing entirely to put it out to sea and hope that it survives the punishing wind and waves—and performs as expected. Annette and her team turned to making their prototypes more robust to get ready for ocean testing. They integrated stronger materials, like fiberglass, with more reinforcements.

The students began joking: "If there's a national disaster, we're all gonna climb inside this thing, because whatever happens, whatever might fall on us, we'll all be OK."

But then the team realized something. The design was certainly stronger, but it was a lot heavier, too. "We didn't have the buoyancy to prevent this thing from sinking," she says.

Annette von Jouanne stands atop the float of one of the wave-energy device prototypes her team helped design and build with Columbia Power Technologies.

So they went back to the drawing board, this time to make their design more buoyant. They added extra flotation material all around the device. "We hoped and prayed it would work," she says.

In October 2007, their device (nicknamed SeaBeav1, after Oregon State's mascot, the beaver) was ready. The team was excited to see how SeaBeav1 would do in the ocean, but the weather was too stormy. While they waited for rough winds to die down, they tested SeaBeav1's stability off a pier in the Yaquina Bay.

During the bay testing, they were able to get only minor motion between the spar and the float. They checked the forecast again and again, hoping for a break in the weather so they could take SeaBeav1 out into some more energetic waves.

Finally, the weather cleared. On October 13, about a week later than they had planned, Annette and her team met on the Newport Marina docks. Using a crane, the team lowered the device into the water and hooked it up behind

Annette's team lowers SeaBeav1 into the water from the docks in Newport, Oregon, tows it out to sea, and deploys it off the back of the research vessel *Pacific Storm* for testing.

the *Pacific Storm,* Oregon State's eighty-foot-long (24-meter) research vessel. Slowly, carefully, they towed it two and half miles out to sea. There, the *Pacific Storm* and the SeaBeav1 dropped anchors. Still loosely attached to the ship through a power cable, SeaBeav1 rode up and down the swells. Overall, the field testing revealed that the device could produce at least 1 kilowatt—but with some work back at the energy lab, the team increased it to 10 kilowatts. "It was an invaluable deployment," says Annette. "We learned a lot about the buoy and a lot about how to test the electrical output of a device in the ocean without having to run a power cable all the way back to shore."

The team was not ready to leave SeaBeav1 out at sea, even overnight, because they were still developing and testing their mooring system. So they towed the device back to the docks to discuss future testing.

Then another big fall storm blew in, ripping across the coastline and inland, with wind gusts a howling sixty-five miles an hour. The storm stripped leaves from trees, triggered rock falls and small landslides, and knocked out power to tens of thousands of people. Annette and her team decided to delay further ocean testing until the summer and returned SeaBeav1 safely to the lab.

The *Corvallis Gazette-Times* ran an article declaring: "Weather Sinks Wave Buoy Test for Season." Annette couldn't believe they used the word *sink* in the headline. People who glanced at the article assumed that her device had sunk. Just as she was trying to prove the viability of wave energy to the public, government, and funders, the article misled people into thinking that prospects were bleak.

And then, two weeks later, the unthinkable happened to another wave-energy device created by a different team, a disaster that affected everyone.

Not far from where the SeaBeav1 test took place, a Canadian company, Finavera Renewables, was deep into a successful test of their device, called the AquaBuOY.

The team that designed the AquaBuOY was inspired by a clever way South Africans drew water from water tables deep underground more than a century ago using a hose pump. They threaded a hose underground and secured it to the bottom of the water table. After the hose filled with water, they closed off the bottom and pulled the hose taut. The hose would stretch and narrow. (It's like those woven tube toy finger traps. If you stick your index fingers in each end of the tube and pull them away from each other, the tube narrows and your fingers get stuck.) As the hose stretched and narrowed, it would push water out the opening at the top, thus acting as a hose pump.

The AquaBuOY essentially did the same thing. Hoses submerged underwater stretched and relaxed, stretched and relaxed as a floating buoy on the surface rose and fell with the waves. The moving water spun a turbine, which generated electricity.

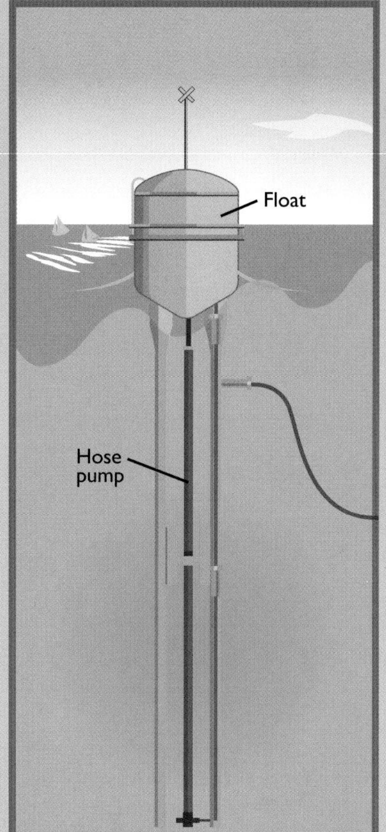


As the yellow AquaBuOY float bobs at the surface of the water, it extends and releases a long hose (blue in the diagram). The narrowing of the hose as it extends thrusts water through a turbine, generating electricity.

# WILD WAVE INVENTIONS OF THE WORLD

Extracting energy from waves is a gnarly engineering challenge—and creative minds from around the globe have come up with a dizzying array of ideas on how to do it. Here is a sampling of ingenious wave devices under development in other countries.

## PELAMIS WAVE MACHINE, SCOTLAND

www.pelamiswave.com

*Resembles:* A cross between a sea snake and a train.

*How it works:* A number of connected tubes, as big as railway cars, float semisubmerged, facing into the waves. As the tubes pitch in the waves, teetering like a seesaw, hydraulic cylinders at the joints pump fluid to drive generators at each joint.

*Fun facts:* Named after the snake *Pelamis platurus,* the machine is painted bright red to make it more visible to nearby ships.

## WAVE DRAGON, DENMARK

www.wavedragon.net; www.tecdragon.pt

*Resembles:* A partially submerged *Starship Enterprise.*

*How it works:* Wave dragon is essentially a floating hydroelectric dam. Walls direct waves up a ramp. The wave overtops, filling a huge reservoir above sea level. Gravity does the rest; water flows back to sea level, spinning turbines.

*Fun facts:* The wave dragon can grow . . . and grow. Because energy generation relies on waves overtopping the device, there is no upper limit to the size of the device and how much energy it can produce. The bigger the reservoir and the more turbines spinning, the more electricity generated.

## AQUAMARINE POWER'S OYSTER 800, SCOTLAND

www.aquamarinepower.com

*Resembles:* A huge opening and closing jaw (or oyster).

*How it works:* Located around 1.3 miles (.5 kilometer) from shore, in depths of around thirty to fifty feet (10 to 15 meters), the Oyster is a huge buoyant flap attached to the sea floor, which pitches back and forth in nearshore waves. The moving flap pushes high pressure fresh water through pipes to the shore, where the moving water spins a hydroelectric turbine, producing electricity.

*Fun facts:* Hinged flaps duck under the biggest waves, just like a surfer, and therefore avoid damage. Also, even though it is a wave device, all the electricity is generated onshore.

## OCEANLINX'S WAVE DEVICES, AUSTRALIA

www.oceanlinx.com

*Resembles:* One design looks like a concrete block with a jet engine on top; another resembles a floating dock with one or more jet engines on top.

*How it works:* A wave hitting the device pushes water up into it. The water pushes the air up, and the moving air spins a wind turbine. When the water recedes, the air reverses direction, spinning the turbine again. This can be done nearshore with a concrete bottom that sits on the sea floor (greenWAVE), on a floating platform (ogWAVE), or as a cluster of floating devices (blueWAVE).

*Fun facts:* None of Oceanlinx's wave devices have any moving parts underwater. Also, since greenWAVEs are stationary and built to withstand pounding waves, they can act as breakwaters, helping protect coasts and harbors.

Many different devices were being created and tested around the world, but AquaBuOY's developers hoped they were a step ahead of the rest. "The race right now is to prove out the technology," said Finavera spokesperson Myke Clark. "The technology that is likely to prevail is the one that produces the most electricity for the lowest cost. . . . Whoever gets to that first and can sell it to a utility . . . that's likely the device that will prevail." The company had high hopes for the AquaBuOY, with plans to generate electricity with arrays of buoys off the coasts of Oregon, Washington, and California within just five years. But first they had to prove its worth in the water. Wave tank tests had gone well, but they needed to see how their half-scale model would do in real swells.

Finavera's AquaBuOY successfully deployed off the Oregon coast in 2007.

About five weeks before Annette's ocean test of SeaBeav1, the Finavera team towed their seventy-five-foot (23-meter) AquaBuOY a couple miles out to sea from Newport, Oregon, and tethered it to the ocean floor.

The AquaBuOY performed beautifully for months, smoothly riding the waves, stretching and squeezing the hose, moving pressurized water forcefully enough to generate an estimated 250 kilowatts of electricity, enough to power up to 250 homes.

"It performed exactly as we thought it would perform," said Myke Clark.

Engineers monitored the AquaBuOY remotely using wireless and satellite technology. They worried when the fall storms that delayed Annette's tests pummeled their device. "We were so pleased that the AquaBuOY survived the storms just fine and the technology worked so well," says Alla Weinstein, the entrepreneur who brought the technology to Finavera.

Then at the end of October, the engineers noticed something. A bilge pump, designed to drain any water leaking into the float, had turned on. "We knew the pump had kicked in so we knew that water was coming in," Alla says. "But we didn't know how much water the float was taking in and whether or not the bilge pump was keeping up."

The AquaBuOY testing was scheduled to end the next day, so engineers motored out to inspect and prepare it for towing. Seas were calm and the device looked OK except that it was sitting a little low in the water. “Good thing we’re taking it out tomorrow,” everyone agreed.

But they were too late. That night the AquaBuOY sank.

The $2 million device plunged 115 feet and settled on the ocean floor.

Everyone was stunned.

Finavera tried to take it in stride. “It was a prototype,” Myke Clark said, “and issues arise with prototypes sometimes. This was not going to be the device we would use in a commercial wave project, which clearly would have gone through a lot more testing, including survivability tests.”

But fishers, crabbers, and environmentalists worried that the device sitting on the sea floor would poison habitat and tangle up their gear. “I know there may be concerns about environmental impacts, but part of the benefit of the design of the device is there are no hydraulic oils,” Myke Clark said. “There is little if any environmental impact from having this down there. Basically it is metal with a piece of rubber hose in it.”

Finavera had agreed that everything they put in the water, they would take out. And they did. It was a multimillion-dollar effort to yank the sunken buoy off the ocean floor and haul it back to shore. But nine months after it sank, they did it.

“The fishing community was extremely pleased,” says Annette. “Even that devastating loss ended up being really an encouragement that, wow, worst-case scenario did happen and they did extract it.”

The sinking ultimately brought down the AquaBuOY. A few years after the incident, Finavera called off their Washington and California wave energy projects. And in 2010, Finavera sold off the part of the company dedicated to wave energy to focus only on wind power.

“When you’re engineering something new, you need to have failures to learn from them, but investors don’t handle failure well,” says Alla. “The sad thing about the AquaBuOY is that the sinking had nothing to do with the wave energy technology. The engineering of the hose-pump mechanism worked perfectly. But the reality and the lesson here is that everything around the technology—the housing, the float, the bilge pumps, the moorings—has to be perfect, too. The repercussions for something not working in the water are just so severe.”

But the failure hurt more than just Finavera. When Annette talked about her buoy, people asked: But didn’t it sink? Because the buoy was near her test site in the same season, her work was sometimes associated with that devastating failure. The bad publicity also spooked potential wave energy funders and investors.

The sinking drove home for other ocean energy innovators the risks of working in the ocean. They knew they absolutely had to get everything right. But they wouldn’t give up. “We couldn’t let the AquaBuOY sinking stop us,” Annette says. “It’s just one of those things where you just have to persevere.”

In June 2008, the Environmental Protection Agency’s ocean survey vessel *Bold* took this image of Finavera’s sunken AquaBuOY on the ocean floor using a high-resolution sidescan sonar. Pinpointing the location of the buoy aided in its recovery.

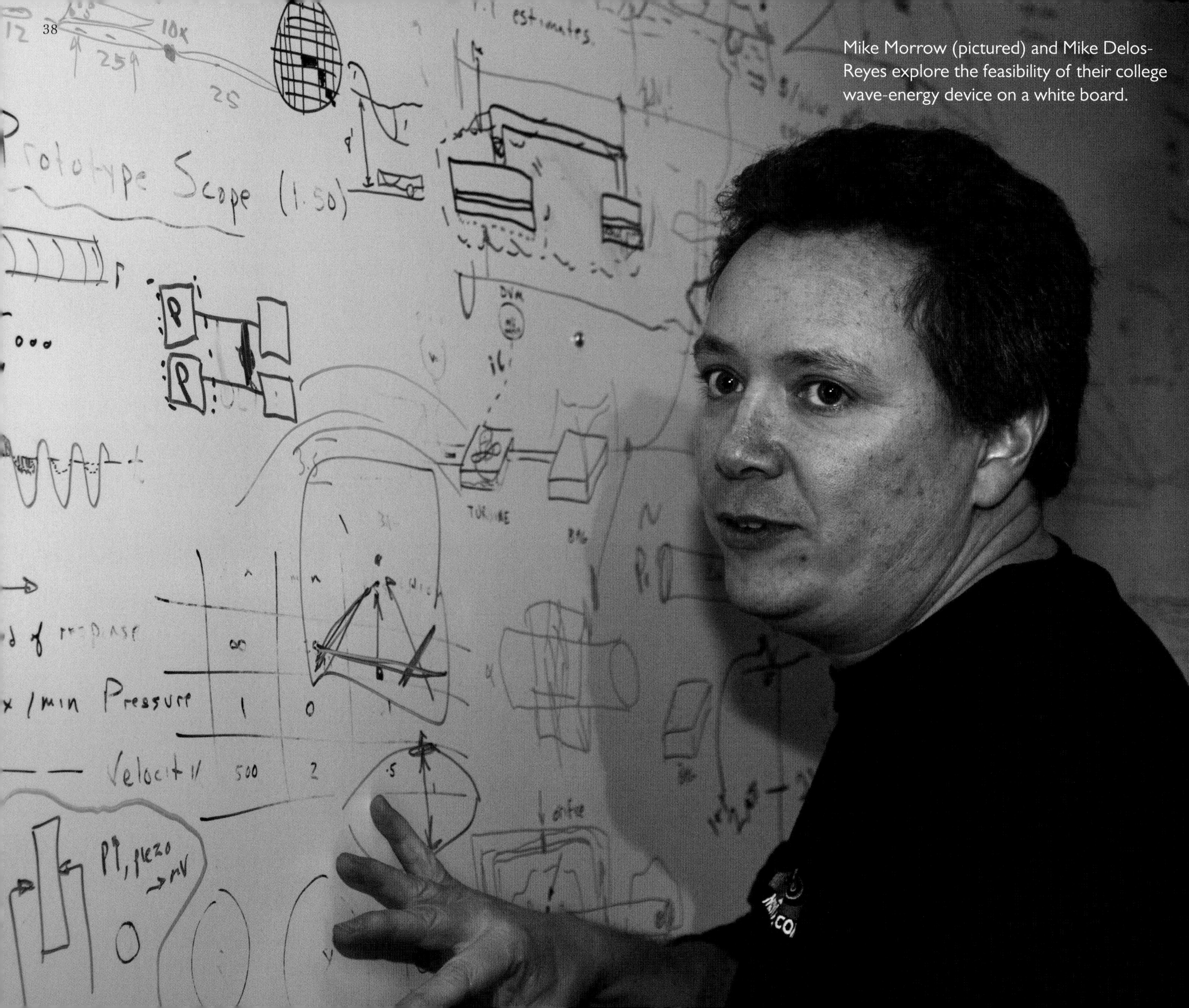


Mike Morrow (pictured) and Mike Delos-Reyes explore the feasibility of their college wave-energy device on a white board.

5

# Ducking the Waves

More than a dozen years after boxing up their ocean-floor wave-energy device, Mike Morrow and Mike Delos-Reyes discussed the sinking of the AquaBuOY. "Yeah, ours would never sink," Mike Delos-Reyes chuckled. "It would already be on the ocean floor."

The Mikes were working as engineers at Hewlett-Packard, and they began to reminisce about their college project. They wondered: Could their invention ever really produce electricity in a cost-effective way? They began reading up on the field. "I was, frankly, incredulous that nobody had pursued anything even remotely like what we had developed," says Mike Morrow. "It was one of those 'All right, darn it, if you guys aren't going to do anything with this technology then we'll just have to do it ourselves' moments."

The Mikes found an empty conference room with a big dry-erase board. Now, with forty years' engineering experience between them, they took a new look at their old idea. A device on the ocean floor has some real advantages over devices that bob in the waves. Big storms, huge rogue waves, even tsunamis are not likely to damage a device 50 to 120 feet (15 to 37 meters) underwater. No buoys or elaborate mooring system would be needed. Hidden underwater and invisible from the surface, it wouldn't affect anyone's ocean views. Boats, including fishing vessels, could pass right over it without damaging either the boats or the device.

Since the Mikes' wave device sits on the ocean floor, whales and other marine animals could travel over it without running into anything.

A fishing boat leaves Newport Marina for its trawling grounds. Boats should be able to pass right over the Mikes' wave device on the ocean floor.

# STUDYING SEA CREATURES

Because harnessing wave energy is so new, no one really knows how it will affect marine animals or the environment. No doubt wave energy projects will introduce large machines and other structures such as anchors and cables to the ocean. Birds could collide with the buoys, and marine mammals could become entangled in cables. Items on the seafloor or rising up from the bottom may create artificial reefs that could attract new species of fish to the area. This could be good or bad; such reefs could improve local biodiversity or introduce nonnative species. To study these impacts, researchers are observing and comparing the movement of marine animals in the area before, during, and after devices are installed.

The projects may also introduce new sounds and electromagnetic fields to the sea. Wave-energy devices, as well as cables that take electricity to shore, can emit electromagnetic fields. And mooring cables can thrum in the currents, like guitar strings. Researchers have just begun to measure these disturbances and study whether they affect whales, sharks, dolphins, salmon, rays, crabs, and other marine animals that use electromagnetism and sound for feeding, mating, or navigation.

Wave-energy devices will also take something away from the environment—some of the energy from waves. Reduced wave power could affect currents, sand movement, water temperature, and water mixing near the shore. Initial studies of the Oregon coast suggest wave-energy devices will not notably add or erode sand from beaches. But smaller changes could affect feeding or reproduction of tiny creatures.

Marine biologists have just begun to study how wave-energy devices will affect marine animals such as these sea lions.

Wave energy pioneers like the Mikes and Annette are eager to learn more about how their machines affect marine animals. And they are developing their inventions with sea creatures in mind, trying to minimize sound and electromagnetic emissions and even exploring how paint colors and patterns affect plants and animals. "The last thing I want to do is harm the ocean and its beautiful creatures," Annette says.

A machine on the ocean floor faces other challenges, though. There's less energy available on the bottom of the sea than on the surface. Also, ocean water transports sand, which could pile up on the device or hollow out the ocean floor beneath it. Mussels, barnacles, and other sea animals and plants might grow on it. No one knows how the device would affect other sea creatures, though it seems unlikely that whales or other mobile marine animals would bump into it.

Still, the Mikes thought, it was worth a serious try.

So they made a list of steps they needed to take:

1. Run the idea by some experts: A professor who had served on their senior project committee had become active in the wave energy field and thought the idea had promise. Check.
2. Bring on a partner, someone who knew business: A fellow HP employee named Mike Miller. Check.
3. Form a company: M3 Wave Energy Systems, named after the three Mikes. Check.
4. Perfect the prototype: Well, that was going to be a lot tougher.

To make and test a decent prototype they needed the same two things Annette needed: money and somewhere to test. They checked to see if the old wave flume from Graf Hall was available. It had disappeared, either into the trash or into someone's backyard. But Mike Morrow had just remodeled his house. Walking around the construction debris, he saw old beams, plywood, and cement blocks that could make the bones of a wave flume. The Mikes dragged the materials into an old barn on the property and started to do what they do best: building.

Over the course of a few weeks, they fashioned a thirty-three-foot (10-meter) long flume out of plywood lined with thick plastic from Home Depot. They added a Plexiglas window so they could watch their device. But the Plexiglas bulged from the weight of the water and sprung a leak onto the gravel floor. "We sweated over the leaking for a little while," Mike Morrow says. "Until we realized: 'Hey, who cares if it leaks! If too much water drips out, we'll just refill it!'"

It wasn't pretty, but it worked. "Now M3 Wave Energy Systems has the largest private wave flume in the Northwest," Mike Morrow says. Then he grins. "Of course, it's probably the only private wave flume in the Northwest."

Mike Delos-Reyes examines the wave flume he and Mike Morrow built in Morrow's shed.

The Mikes envision clusters of DMPs on the ocean floor.

Mike Morrow stands on the sturdy truck trailer that became the backbone of the $^{1}/_{6}$-scale DMP.

They perfected the design of their device, now called the Delos-Reyes Morrow Pressure Device, or DMP. With all the increased interest in wave energy, the U.S. Department of Energy and the Oregon Wave Energy Trust were offering development grants. Based on their work in their homemade wave flume, the Mikes won the grants. It was a dream come true. They would be able to build a real $^{1}/_{6}$-scale model and finally give their invention a true test at the O. H. Hinsdale Large Wave Flume.

Of course, milk bags, plywood, and plastic crates wouldn't do for a thirty-foot-long (9 meters) device that would face the equivalent of thirty-foot-high (9 meters) waves. The Mikes wanted a strong steel platform to act as the base for their device. They knew they would have to transport the device from Mike Morrow's backyard to Hinsdale on a truck. When they were considering what size trailer they would need, they had a "eureka" moment. What if they made the platform out of a truck trailer? They visited a local trailer seller and sketched out what they would need: a street-legal car-haul trailer with room cut out for the two bags and the turbine and modified to be used with Hinsdale's crane lift. Then their device could both drive down the highway and sit on the wave flume floor.

They started making air bags of different shapes and sizes in Mike Morrow's barn. They settled on a design eight feet by four feet (2.4 by 1.2 meters) made out of a strong material used by firefighters to store huge amounts of water at remote sites.

Mike Delos-Reyes works on the air bags for the 1/6-scale prototype DMP.

The Mikes' print-on-demand bidirectional air turbine for the 1/6-scale DMP.

They found pipes that could withstand winds of up to eighty miles per hour, so the air whooshing from bag to bag wouldn't shatter the pipes. Finally, they needed a real turbine, not something made with plastic spoons. On the Internet they found some drawings for a bidirectional air turbine. They loaded the plans into a computer-aided design (CAD) program. Then they printed the turbine in 3-D in plastic. The cost—just four hundred bucks.

After work and on weekends, the Mikes built parts in Mike Morrow's barn and assembled everything in his backyard. They decided to leave the turbine off for the first tests in the Hinsdale flume. Computer models predicted the device would generate air speeds as high as eighty miles per hour. "We were afraid the power would just blast the turbine to bits," Mike Morrow says.

Then they drove off to Hinsdale.

When the Mikes pulled up with their trailer/wave-energy device, the staff didn't know what to think. They hadn't seen anything like it before.

As the Mikes started lowering the street-safe trailer into the flume, someone asked: "Aren't you worried about your brake lights?" But the Mikes were too excited to start testing. "Let's just do it," Mike Morrow said. "We'll deal with anything that breaks when the time comes."

The DMP secured in place at the bottom of the mostly empty O. H. Hinsdale wave flume.

They lowered the DMP to the bottom of the concrete flume and bolted the trailer to the concrete wall. Then they started to fill the flume with water.

While chatting with a professor who had come to observe, Mike Morrow stopped midsentence. "Hold on," he said. "There are bubbles—bubbles streaming from our bags." Water filling up their air bags could mean game over.

The Mikes discussed draining the flume and checking the leak. But it takes half a day to fill the flume, and they had to pay $3,000 a day whether they did any testing or not. The Mikes agreed: "Let's just let it ride."

They filled the flume to eight feet (2.4 meters). Then they turned on the waves.

WHOOOSH! The wave generator sent the first wave. WHOOOSH! And another. WHOOOSH! And another.

As the waves passed over the DMP, the bags pushed the air back and forth, back and forth. The velocity meter showed the wind speed rising from twenty to thirty miles an hour.

They turned up the waves, higher and higher, until the flume was making the biggest waves it could. The waves roared in thunderous, tumbling blasts. Air moved powerfully back and forth from bag to bag. The velocity meter maxed out at seventy-two miles an hour.

"Awesome, just awesome," Mike Morrow said. At full scale, the 120-foot by 40-foot device (37 by 12 meters) could generate about 150 kilowatts of electricity. Arrays of ten devices would generate an impressive 1.5 megawatts, enough to power 1,500 homes.

When they drained the flume and checked the bags, they were bone dry inside. The air pressure had kept the water out. And the trailer brake lights? They survived just fine.

Maybe, just maybe, their idea could really work.

It was time to make more than just wind—it was time to make power. The Mikes drained the flume and swapped in the 3-D plastic turbine. The voltmeter confirmed that the device actually generated electricity. The Mikes were thrilled, but they wanted proof they could see with their own eyes. It was December, so they rigged up some red LED lights and started the waves. Their DMP lit up the Christmas tree.

The waves rolling over the 1/6-scale DPM light a Christmas tree.

The Newport Marina in Oregon, launching spot for fishing boats and wave-energy device tests.

6

# Testing, Testing

It's a sparkling blue day in August 2012. As the twenty-four-foot (7 meter) fishing boat *Muleskinner* chugs out of the Newport (Oregon) Marina, the air is rich with a salty, marshy, fishy scent. Pelicans soar past the bow, seagulls scream overhead, and halyards clank in the breeze.

Annette von Jouanne and graduate student Terry Lettenmeier are headed out into the Pacific Ocean toward yet another wave-energy device bobbing in the waves. But it's not Annette's device. In recent years, her mission has shifted from creating new technologies that demonstrate the promise of commercial wave energy to supporting developers as they advance their inventions toward utility-scale use. (She is still working with students to develop lower-power devices for remote uses, such as running self-powered marine monitoring buoys like tsunami early-warning systems.)

Annette knows from experience that a crucial step in the development of any wave-energy device is testing in the ocean. Researchers need to check how the mooring system works; how the device performs; how it is affected by things like seaweed, barnacle growth, and salty water; and how it affects the environment around it. They need to watch how their inventions handle the tumultuous seas—even on a calm day, devices will be tossed and tugged by sideswiping waves and strong currents.

Although testing off the back of the *Pacific Storm* worked well for Annette in the early years, research vessels are expensive to run. A crew has to monitor the boat, the device, and the cables connecting them all day and all night. "I wanted to explore the mobile ocean test berth concept and figure out a way to hook a device to an instrumentation buoy and leave it there to do its work and collect data," Annette says. So Annette and her colleagues created a buoy, called the Ocean Sentinel, and packed it with important instruments so developers all around the world could come and test their devices.

The Ocean Sentinel in dry dock before being deployed in the ocean.

## TESTING WELCOME

Since 2004, Annette von Jouanne had dreamed of offering a national center to support the work of ocean energy developers from all over the globe. She wanted the center to include . . .

- Oregon State University's energy lab
- a wave energy linear test bed that mimics the motion of waves to test devices on land
- the O. H. Hinsdale Wave Research Laboratory, including the wave flume and the tsunami wave basin for scaled testing
- the Hatfield Marine Science Center for environmental research
- ocean test berths where developers could test at sea

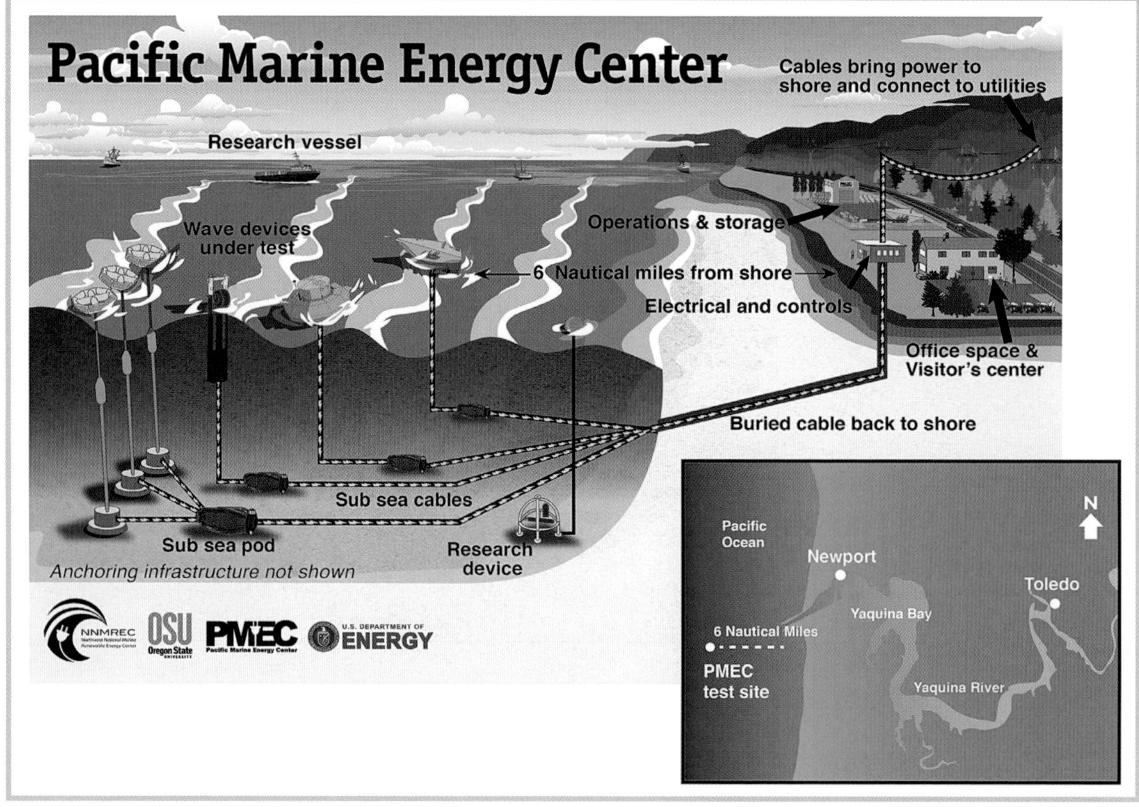


In 2008, her vision became a reality. The Northwest National Marine Renewable Energy Center (NNMREC), one of three national centers, is a partnership between OSU, with a focus on wave energy research, and the University of Washington, which focuses on tidal energy (harnessing the in and out flow of the tides and resulting currents). NNMREC is working to develop four ocean berths where companies can test wave-energy devices or arrays of devices large enough to be used by a utility, such as a local or regional power company. The berths, located approximately five miles out in the ocean, will each have a cable on the sea floor that can bring electricity from the tests to shore to help fill local energy needs. Fees charged to companies to use the berths will support deployment and maintenance of the test sites—a small price to pay for valuable ocean experience.

The WET-NZ wave-energy device on its side in dry dock. When deployed, the buoy will sit vertically in the water, with only the yellow portion visible.

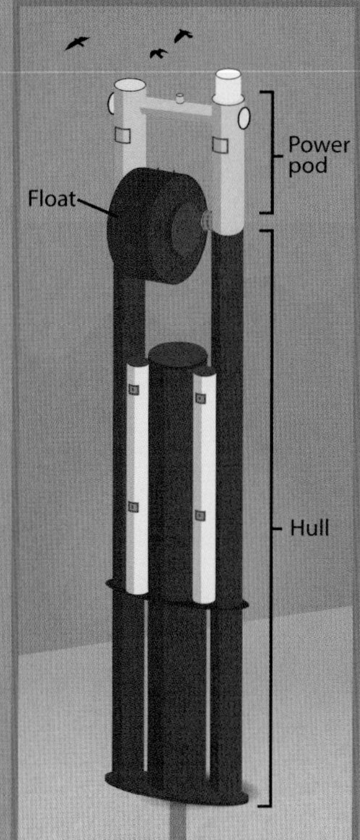


This diagram shows the three main parts of the WET-NZ device. The hull is flooded with sea-water to add mass to hold the device steady in the waves. The float moves with the waves pivoting on a single axle at the waterline. Power conversion equipment in the Power Pod turns the movement of the float into electricity.

The first user of the Ocean Sentinel test berth was New Zealand's WET-NZ, which stands for Wave Energy Technology—New Zealand. The hull of the WET-NZ is weighted with seawater to keep it low in the water and stable. A big float on the device moves up and down, so the float creates motion relative to the stable hull. Machinery in the device converts this relative motion to electricity. The float also surges forward and back and side to side, so that passing seawater is also converted into electricity. An innovative design allows the device to survive rough waters by lying down and letting the biggest waves pass over it.

The WET-NZ begins to rise from its horizontal position to its vertical position.

Several prototypes of the WET-NZ have already been tested off the New Zealand coast. The device fared well in several nasty storms, but engineers wanted to increase the amount of power the WET-NZ could extract. So, they came to the United States to test three float designs in the Hinsdale lab: the original pizza-wedge shape, a cylindrical shape, and a diamond shape. The cylinder looked the most promising, so engineers redesigned the device and built a half-scale model to test at sea. "Annette's test berth gave us an easy way to do that," says Justin Klure, a consultant with Northwest Energy Innovations, which managed the WET-NZ deployment. Annette's team helped with permitting and deployment, gathered power data for the WET-NZ engineers, and helped monitor the device in the water.

Now Annette and her team are heading out to check on the WET-NZ and the test equipment. The boat, the *Muleskinner,* passes the jetty and enters open water. Whitecaps glow like snowy peaks. Chuck Pavlik, a member of FINE (Fishermen Involved in Natural Energy) who is piloting the boat, cranks its throttle, and it shoots forward, nose pointing to the sky like a speedboat.

SWOOOSH! The boat plows up a face of wave.

BAM! It smacks back down into the trough, white water spraying up both sides.

The boat barrels up another wave face. SWOOOOSH!

This time, at the top of the wave, everyone braces themselves.

BAM! The boat drops into the trough, a wake foaming up behind.

Bait hooks hanging in the cabin tinkle and clatter like chimes as Annette peers out the windows, trying to get her bearings. "I think we need to head farther north toward the lighthouse," she says. From the benches inside the cabin she can't see much but white water spraying up. "Do you have the GPS coordinates?" she asks Chuck. "I have them here if you need them."

Annette and her colleagues are looking for the temporary test site, a one-square-mile swath of ocean marked with bright yellow buoys. As the boat plows up the side of a wave, the bow faces up and all anyone can see out the front window is sky. BAM! When it hits the trough, all anyone can see is the face of the next wave.

Even though these are just small sum-

Chuck Pavlik piloting Annette and her team to the test site on his fishing boat.

Close-up of the TRIAXYS riding a wave.

mer swells, everyone onboard, except Chuck, is pale and looking around nervously. Someone offers motion sickness medication, and a few queasy people take it. Others sip ginger ale to settle their stomachs. People try to lock their eyes on the horizon, when they can catch a glimpse of it between waves.

As the boat heads up a wave, Chuck assesses his passengers.

"Anyone who feels queasy can go out back . . ."

BAM!

". . . and get some fresh air."

As the boat approaches the northwest side of the test site, Annette and Terry spot something. "Could be the TRIAXYS," she says. The TRIAXYS is a buoy that measures the magnitude, period (the time between two crests), and direction of the waves and the current. Placed just inside the test site, it gathers essential information about the waves experienced by the device being tested. But the TRIAXYS is small enough to be hard to see from a boat. Similar monitoring buoys have been hit in past deployments, so Annette wants to check how this one is faring.

Everyone peers out, scanning the chop for the little buoy as the boat rides to the top of a wave. "There!" Annette points, and the pilot cuts the engine. Riding low in the swells, with waves splashing over it and current rippling behind it, the TRIAXYS looks like a cross between R2D2 and a jellyfish.

Annette and Terry move aft and lean over the edge of the boat. Annette's hair whips in the wind. They examine the clear dome with solar panels inside, looking for scuff marks, dings, cracks, or scratches. "You know what? It looks good!" Terry says.

Annette looks relieved. "It doesn't look like anything hit it."

Chuck's boat enters the test site, its four corners marked with what look like big yellow bouncy balls. Everyone begins to scan the area for marine animals. A flock of sandpipers flit by. A few ducks bob in the water. Seagulls paddle around and call overhead.

The scientists and fisherman are not just casually watching wildlife. As wave-energy devices get closer to commercial deployment, everyone wants to know how marine animals and the marine environment are affected by them. A radar screen near Chuck's steering wheel lights up with a big blob of light green and red dots. "Check it out . . . it's a whole school of fish, probably coho salmon, heading for the river," he says. But no one sees any seals, sea lions, porpoises, or whales.

The scientists will search for and note all the marine mammals they see today. They'll be back at least every two weeks to observe, and onsite cameras will snap pictures at least every ten minutes. Annette and her colleagues have offered the test site to be used for other animal and environmental studies as well.

Chuck's depth finder also shows fish underwater as green or red dots.

Annette and Terry turn their attention to the WET-NZ, which is jutting up from the sea in the center of the site. It looks like two thick yellow telephone poles with a large brick-red cylindrical float in the middle that heaves up and down in the waves. At half scale, the thing is still massive—a whopping 65 feet (20 meters) tall. And even though more than 130 feet (40 meters) of it is underwater, where most of the machine can interact with the passing waves, close up the device still looks huge.

Chuck slows the boat and Annette and Terry head to the aft deck for a better look at the device. The float slowly moves in the waves. Bracing himself against the boat to keep the camera steady, Terry takes a video of the wave device's motion.

"You have it pretty heavily loaded, right?" Annette asks Terry.

He nods. Using remote control, the team is able to vary how freely the float moves. "Heavily loaded" means restricting the float so that it makes small, slow movements with more torque. Engineers need to find out which generates more power: heavy loading or letting the float move freely and quickly. "It'll be good to compare the video to data on the power generated," Terry says.

A cable connects the WET-NZ to something that looks like a bright yellow eighteen-foot (6-meter) barge. It's the Ocean Sentinel. Wave-energy device developers need to know how much electricity their device generates, so the Ocean Sentinel collects this information. But as

The WET-NZ device being towed off the Oregon coast. Next it's on its way for testing in Hawaii.

The WET-NZ rides a wave off the coast off Newport, Oregon.

The Ocean Sentinel collects information about how a wave-energy device performs and sends the information to shore.

wave-energy devices get closer to commercial reality, they also have to understand how the electricity will be absorbed into the electrical grid, which merges power from various sources and doles it out to homes and businesses. The Ocean Sentinel acts like a power grid, and can both absorb and provide power to the wave-energy devices under test.

"Everything looks fine," Annette says as she scans the WET-NZ, the Ocean Sentinel, and the cable connecting them. For the six-week test, everything performs beautifully, with WET-NZ demonstrating a 20-kilowatt capacity rating. Long before the onslaught of violent fall and winter storms, the teams tow the Ocean Sentinel, the WET-NZ, and all the mooring and testing equipment back to shore.

The next stop for the WET-NZ on its way to commercial deployment: a year of open-water testing in Hawaiian waters. The group is eager to conduct a longer test, with time to make adjustments, without the costs of trying to survive in dangerous Oregon winter seas. "Twenty-foot swells make me nervous," jokes Justin. "I'd hate to have to check every morning to see if sixty-foot swells were on the way."

But if wave energy inventors want to place their devices year-round in waters with the biggest energy punch, eventually they must answer a big question: Can their inventions survive the pummeling, punishing forces of the stormiest seas? And can they generate enough power at the same time to make it all worthwhile?

The waves generated in the tsunami basin of the O. H. Hinsdale Wave Research Laboratory are so authentic that they can be surfed.

7

# Big Power from Big Seas

Ken Rhinefrank, Joe Prudell, and Al Schacher were three of the many Oregon State University students who worked with Annette to develop her first ocean-tested wave energy prototype, SeaBeav1. Al was drawn to wave energy because his big brother was Annette's very first graduate student to work on the project. "I couldn't help but follow in his footsteps," Al says with a smile. Joe, a surfer who grew up in Santa Cruz, California, knew the power of waves firsthand, so joining the project was just another way to revel in the ocean environment he loved so much. And Ken had always had a keen interest in, not wave, but wind energy. "But there was so much excitement around wave energy, so many interesting questions," he says. "I wanted to help develop this untapped source of renewable energy."

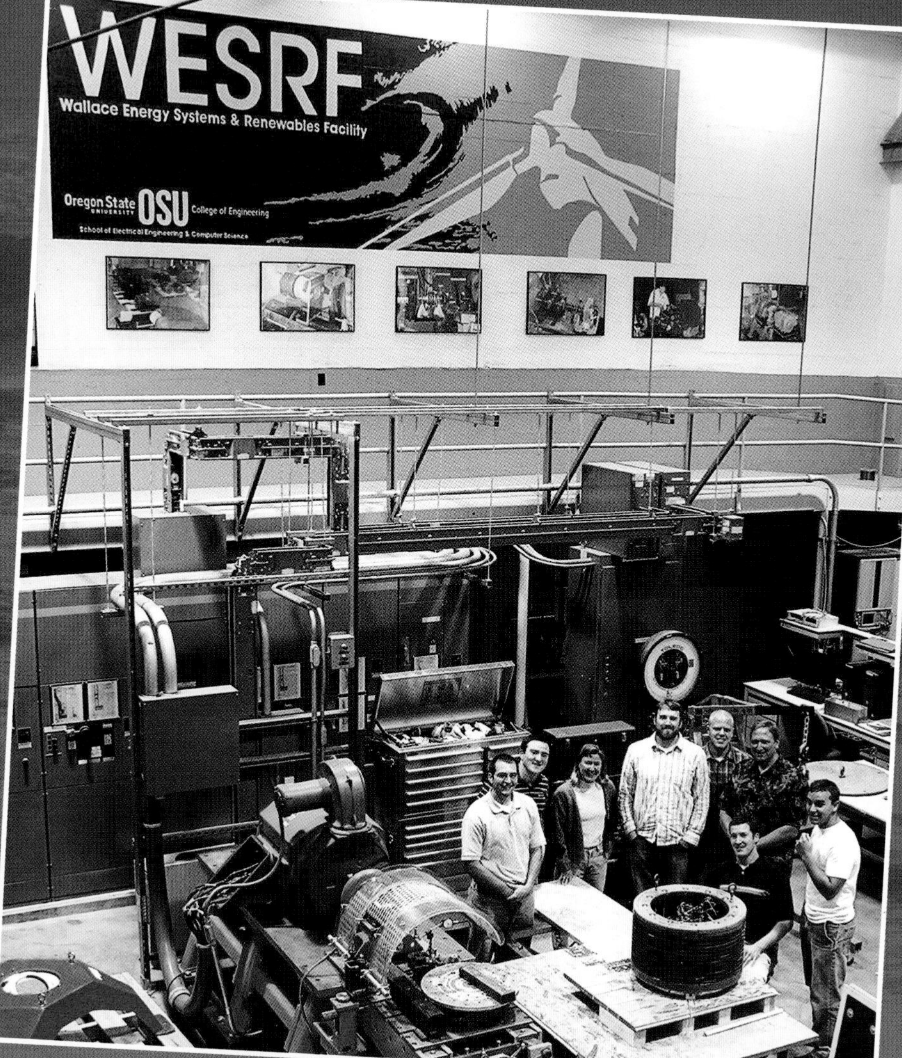


Annette von Jouanne with her team in Oregon State University's power lab WESRF, referred to fondly as "we surf." From the right: Al Schacher, Joe Prudell (seated), Ken Rhinefrank, Ean Amon, Ted Brekken, Annette von Jouanne, Chad Stillinger, Adam Brown.

A company called Columbia Power Technologies was so impressed with the work of Annette's team that they offered Ken, Joe, and Al jobs to continue designing devices. Columbia Power began their foray into wave energy by collaborating with Oregon State University and the U.S. Navy to build on what they'd learned from SeaBeav1. The result was BlueRAY. A six-day test off the back of the *Pacific Storm* in 2008 was a real eye-opener for Ken, who is now the vice president of research for Columbia Power Technologies. "Even though the biggest waves were just eight or nine feet, small for the Oregon coast, they didn't feel small," he says. "Getting hammered by those waves gave us a renewed appreciation for the engineering challenge of surviving in the ocean environment. It's one thing to design for the ocean. It's another to experience it."

But the test was exciting, too. The engineers could see from the back of the boat how well their device performed. As BlueRAY bobbed in the waves, it powered a 1.5-kilowatt navigational light that glowed day and night.

Columbia Power wanted a lot more energy, though. They redesigned their device again and again to find the best way to convert the up-and-down motion of waves into a spinning motion to turn a generator. Once they found a design they liked, they built a 1/7-scale model, called SeaRAY, and deployed it out in the Puget Sound near Seattle. "It was a hard thing to do," Ken says, "like kicking a baby bird out of the nest. When you're testing a device behind a vessel, you're only fifty yards away and you can investigate or fix anything you see. In the Puget Sound, we had to just leave it there."

SeaRAY, a 1/7-scale model, being readied for deployment. The full-scale model would be seven times bigger.

SeaRAY was successfully tested off in the Puget Sound near Seattle for more than year.

Researchers use the tsunami basin to test, among other things, how the shape and spacing of buildings affects how they might fare in a tsunami. Here a simulated tsunami crashes into a scale-model version of the town of Seaside, Oregon.

And leave it they did, for more than a year. The SeaRAY showed the potential to generate 220 kilowatts, which could continuously power close to 220 homes. Watching SeaRAY bob and lurch in the waves gave the engineers lots of ideas about how to make their device even sturdier and more efficient. They redesigned once again.

Now they have a new device, one that they think will outperform all the rest. Dubbed StingRAY, it has two floats and one main body that all move independently: the central body (nacelle), one forward (or front) float, and one aft (or back) float. The more the floats move relative to the nacelle, the more electricity StingRAY generates.

The Columbia Power team has gathered at the O. H. Hinsdale Tsunami Basin, excited, hopeful, and nervous to see how this newest prototype will perform. The tsunami basin (another part of the Hinsdale lab) is a giant shed, like an airplane hangar, with a shallow concrete basin about the length and width of an Olympic swimming pool. Engineers often fill the basin with small-scale model towns, villages, or cities to test how well buildings and bridges withstand tsunamis (huge devastating waves caused mostly by earthquakes). The tests also help them plan evacuation routes and other life-saving strategies. But it turns out the basin is also an excellent place to test how wave-energy devices fare in monster waves.

Columbia Power's Erik Hammagren (right) and Joe Prudell lower StingRAY into the tsunami basin.

The Columbia Power engineers are testing a 33-scale device, which means that the device is 1/33 the size of what the final device will be. So to test it, they have to scale the waves, too. Testing in water 4.5 feet (1.37 meters) deep will replicate behavior in water thirty-three times deeper, or 148 feet (45 meters).

From their five years of experience designing and testing devices, the team is pretty confident that the StingRAY will float properly and that it will move well in the waves. But will this design, with a more streamlined front float and thicker back float, generate more movement and thus more electricity? How much? "We're hoping StingRAY gives us *twice* as much electricity generation as our last design," Ken says.

As far as they know, everyone testing floating wave-energy devices is using a three-point mooring system, which means their devices are held in place with three cables. The Columbia Power engineers are testing a new idea: a single mooring, one cable that connects the front of the device to one marine buoy. That way the device would be free to turn itself into the waves as the waves change direction. "We think it might be more efficient, so that StingRAY gets the best of every wave," says Ken. "It could increase survivability, too, because the device would be facing into the wave properly instead of being slammed from the side." But no one has ever tried this, so they don't really know if it will work. "We do this kind of testing to confirm our ideas before building larger, more expensive devices," Ken says.

In the center of the tsunami basin, StingRAY is lit up like a small radio tower. Poles lined with red LED lights will help the team track the exact movement of StingRAY in the waves. Joe is up to his chest in the 40°F (4°C) water, with only some camouflage waders and a wool hat to warm him. He gently guides StingRAY to a steady position, pointing ninety degrees away from where the waves will come. Slowly, carefully, trying not to stir up a wave that might skew the test, Joe makes his way out of the basin.

Ken speaks into a walkie-talkie to lab manager Tim Maddux in the control room. "First test, 2509, spread zero." Translation: Tim is going to dial up the equivalent of 2.5-meter waves (8 feet) with a 9 second period (meaning nine seconds between the peak of one wave and the peak of the next). Zero spread means that the waves will come evenly from one direction instead of coming at StingRAY from different angles. But at this small scale, we won't see eight-foot waves. More like three inches.

There's a pause, then from Tim: "Intended wave in thirty seconds . . . fifteen seconds . . . start."

Erik (front) and Joe arrange StingRAY's mooring. The LED lights on the poles above StingRAY will help Columbia Power track the device's movement in the waves.

StingRAY rides the waves.

Cha-CHUNK. The whole far wall of the basin kicks out, pushing the water into a wave. Cha-CHUNK . . . cha-CHUNK . . . cha-CHUNK. The wall rhythmically shoves the water, the waves radiate out, and StingRAY starts teeter-tottering in the waves. The waves might look small but StingRAY is small too, so it rocks impressively with the swells.

And StingRAY is doing something else—it's smoothly pivoting from its starting spot and turning to face the waves. "Wow, that was faster than I expected," Ken says.

"Yeah, it hardly took any time at all before it was perfectly positioned," Al adds.

"It really worked," Joe whispers.

The test finishes and they let the waters calm. They ready for the next test, with slightly bigger waves. Tim starts the countdown and the waves head for StingRAY. The waves jostle StingRAY and it pitches forward and aft, the front float bobbing wildly.

"That's it . . . that's what we want," Joe says, admiringly.

Ken's radio blares out: "Wait. The front line. Is it tangled?"

"Yeah, it looks crooked and dangling," someone says.

"Stop the test," Ken orders.

As Joe climbs back into his waders and into the chilly water, Ken muses. "That's why we call this research. Real research is when you don't know exactly what will happen and you're facing questions and challenges you've never seen before and have to create solutions as you go."

Joe checks all the lines and nothing is tangled. They decide a line must have been snarled, but cleared itself. So they put StingRAY into position and continue through sets of tests designed to explore every kind of wave StingRAY might face at sea. They also try different configurations of the device, such as positioning the arms that connect the floats in and out of the water and adding different weights to the front and back floats, which affects their position in the water.

After testing all day, every day, for more than a week, the team is finally ready for what they call Extreme Seas Testing. "Our main goal here," Ken says, "is to demonstrate that the device can survive." To be viable for commercial use, StingRAY has to be able to survive in fifty-year storm conditions—meaning that it would survive the biggest storm to hit in an average fifty years. Off the Oregon coast, that means average wave heights of more than forty-seven feet (14.5 meters). But averages can hide some monsters. In a jumble of big waves, where larger waves overtake and swallow up smaller ones, a fifty-year storm could throw a ninety-five-foot (29-meter) wave—higher than a ten-story building.

And that's not all. "The biggest danger is not necessarily the tallest wave," Ken points out. "It depends on where StingRAY is when the big one hits. Is it at an odd angle from the last wave? Is it twisted somehow? Not recovered from the last wave? What direction is the wave coming from? The truth is, we don't know which wave will be the most dangerous."

The team is not quite ready to throw fifty-year Oregon waves at their precious device, so they start with gentler fifty-year Hawaiian waves, the scaled equivalent of twenty-six feet (8 meters). "It's kind of nice that we can work our way up to the biggest waves," Ken says. "We don't get to do that at sea."

It's time to begin. "Ready," Ken says.

Joe Prudell works on StingRAY in the water. The team tested different-shaped arms for the floats.

Cha-CHUNK. The wall pushes a big wave. Cha-CHUNK, and another. Cha-CHUNK, cha-CHUNK. The waves rise up, looming over StingRAY. A large wave catches another and begins to break.

"Here comes one," Joe says.

The wave rises under StingRAY. The device lurches and bobs.

"Whoa!" Al exclaims.

Then another large one comes. "I would be so scared if I was on a boat and saw a wave that tall," says Joe. The team watches, riveted, half leaning in, half bracing themselves, ready to wince.

Splash! The white water pounds StingRAY but it pops back up.

Then a tall, lean wave heads for the device.

"Oh, these are the worst," Joe says. "It'll float up the wall, then drop off the backside. That setup can be a disaster—"

"OH!" people yell as StingRAY shoots up the wall of the wave and then falls down.

Ken Rhinefrank signals to the control room that StingRAY is ready for the next set of waves.

Erik Hammagren, an engineer, monitors the program that helps Columbia Power track the movement of StingRAY in the waves.

The Columbia Power engineers (from left to right) Al Schacher, Erik Hammagren, and Ken Rhinefrank watch as waves pummel StingRAY.

The device has survived the worst waves it might face off the coast of Hawaii in a half century.

Now it's time to hit StingRAY with the biggies—Oregon ocean monsters—average waves the equivalent of 47 feet (14.5 meters) high. Just like in the ocean, the actual wave heights vary as waves catch up to each other. So the biggest waves could be the equivalent of 95 feet (29 meters).

Ken gives the order: "Ready."

Everyone faces the small device floating in the calm water.

There's a pause, then from Tim: "Intended wave in thirty seconds . . . fifteen seconds . . . start."

The basin is surprisingly quiet. The water is still. StingRAY is motionless.

CA-THWACK. The wall moves. SWOOSH. The water moves. CA-THWACK, SWOOSH!

The waves rise up and build and build. StingRAY bobs and jostles. Then a big wave overtakes another wave and a monster rears up.

StingRAY shoots up the face of the wave and bucks at the top.

The lights flicker, but stay on.

Another monster approaches.

"Oh, man," says Ken.

"This could be make or break," whispers Joe.

StingRAY jostles and rises. The water smashes over it. The engineers look relieved.

Then, three big rollers head straight for the device.

"Oh wow!" someone yells.

The first big one hits StingRAY. It bobs and lurches. Right away, another hits. White water sprays over it. Then the third big wall of water hits. StingRAY jerks. The lights blink off. StingRAY disappears.

The engineers hold their breaths.

StingRAY bobs to the surface. The lights blink on.

The engineers nod to each other and smile.

StingRAY survived.

In fifteen days of testing, StingRAY survived everything the engineers threw at it. Near the end of testing, they allowed big waves to flip the front float to the back, where it would be in a more protected position. "It worked beautifully," Ken says. In that safer survival mode, StingRAY would produce less power. But they figured out a way to remotely continue

A big wave roars toward StingRAY.

the rotation full circle underwater, back to its full-power position. "It was pretty neat," Ken says. "We tested it eight times to make sure it worked consistently."

All this testing has boosted Columbia Power's confidence about their present design. "The floats, the center of gravity, it all makes it so much more seaworthy," Ken says. "It handled the storm waves much better than past designs, and the single-point mooring where it can position itself directly into the wave allows us to make more power while saving a lot of money." And the power generation potential is impressive—330 kilowatts, which could power 330 homes. "It can generate more than 500 kilowatts during larger storms," says Ken. "Longer term we expect to make even more improvements and average power will exceed 600 kilowatts." In the future, Ken projects, wave parks with multiple devices could power thousands of homes.

The Columbia Power engineers are ready for the next step, a big one. They're ready to develop a full-scale device, thirty-three times bigger, something that could be deployed commercially, contributing electricity to the grid. "I feel like we're really close," says Ken.

8

# Saved by Waves?

After decades of hard work, a number of wave energy projects have gained powerful momentum, and the field of wave energy is finally reaching a crest. For the first time ever, a wave energy park is expected to make electricity that can power American homes. Ocean Power Technologies (OPT), a company based in New Jersey, is the first ever to win a permit in the United States to generate electricity from ocean waves to be sold for use in homes and businesses.

George W. Taylor, Ocean Power Technologies' cofounder.

OPT's story begins in Australia with a boy named George W. Taylor, who loved to surf. "You get the feeling of the force of the waves when you're out there surfing," he says. "That was buried deep inside of me." George studied engineering and cofounded a company in the United States that began operations in 1994 to create a float that would heave up and down with the waves and convert that

Ocean Power Technologies' PowerBuoy readied for deployment.

movement into electricity. He teamed up with fellow engineer Joe Burns and business expert Charles Dunleavy, who grew up surfing off the New Jersey shore. "A big part of our story is entrepreneurial," Charles says. "We started with nothing but an idea. We raised a lot of money, and that enabled us to develop the idea, develop the technology. But we have also had to change course very dramatically. We've had to stand in front of customers and investors and say, 'This path that we sold you on, that we thought would work, is not going to work. But we have a different path that we think *will* work.'"

Originally, George's idea was to use piezoelectric plastic, a material that generates electricity when stretched and released. After about three years of developing a system with a float that bobs up and down, stretching and releasing bands of this material, they realized this tactic could never generate enough electricity for big commercial projects. "We massively changed our approach," says Charles, who now serves as CEO of the company.

OPT's PowerBuoys still feature a float

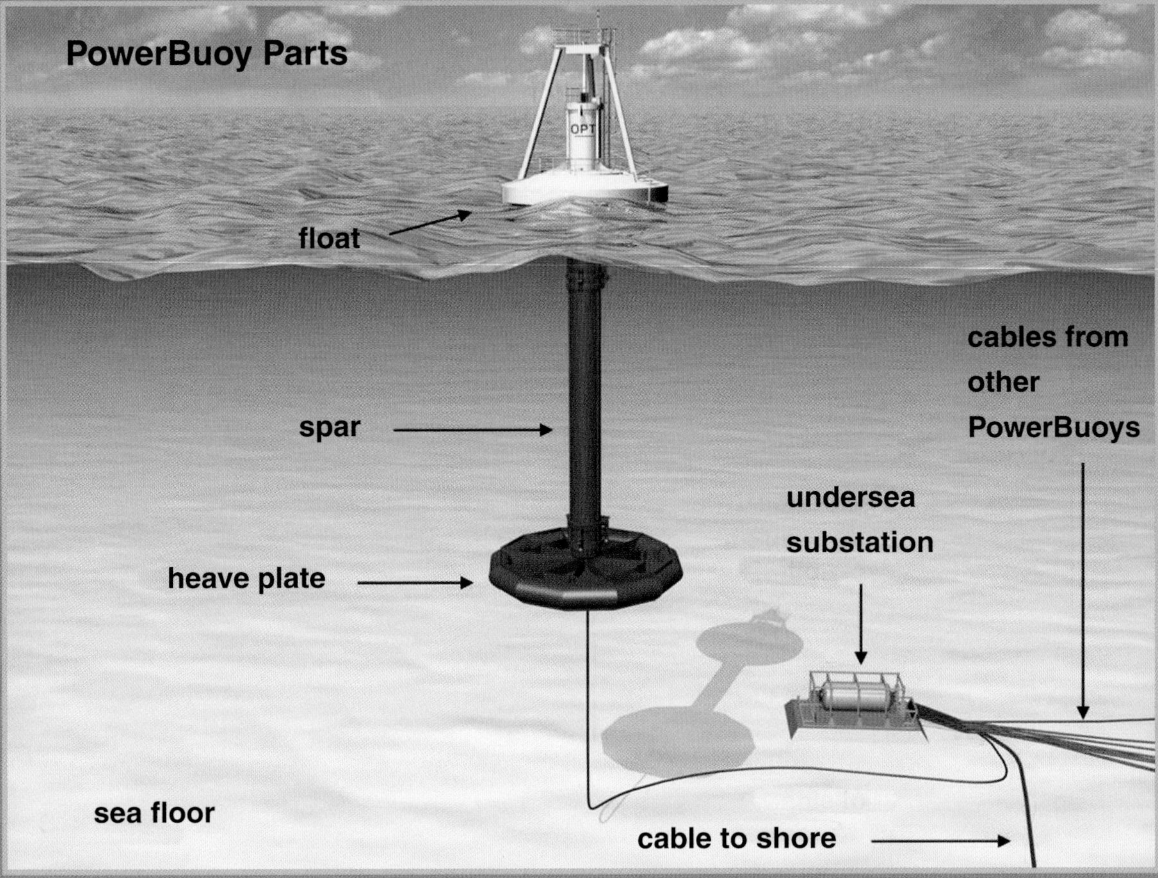


that rises and falls with the waves. But instead of stretching plastic, the movement of the float drives a plunger in the spar up and down. Equipment inside the PowerBuoy converts the vertical motion into rotary motion and the rotary motion drives a generator, making electricity. OPT has even finessed the system to tune the float movement to changing wave conditions. "The float speed actually adjusts in seconds to maximize electricity generation," Charles says.

Like other developers, OPT has tested and refined and tested again. "Job one is surviving whatever Mother Nature throws at us," Charles says. "You're putting a many-ton chunk of metal out in the ocean and subjecting it to tremendous forces. That chunk of metal has to stay put—and has a job to do." OPT prototypes have bobbed off the Atlantic coast on and off for three years, facing storm after storm. A prototype that contributed electricity to a U.S. Marine Corps base in Hawaii weathered waves as high as twenty-two feet (8 meters) from a massive Japanese tsunami. A buoy off the coast of New Jersey withstood

The deployment of the PowerBuoy in Reedsport, Oregon, will follow the same steps as earlier deployments like this one in Scotland. After moorings are anchored, the PowerBuoy is towed out to position and ballasted to an upright position.

monster waves from Hurricane Irene—up to fifty-one feet (16 meters) high.

"We like big waves," says Charles. "Big waves mean big power. But if they get too big, our buoy goes into lockdown." That means that instead of letting the float move up and down around the spar, the whole things moves together as one piece. "Marine buoys have been behaving that way for more than a hundred years, so though waves may go over our buoy and toss it around, history is on our side," says Charles. "We have a high level of confidence that our buoy will survive."

OPT is ready to demonstrate what their Mark 3 PowerBuoy can do in Ore-

gon's strong Pacific Ocean environment. "We're very proud to have received the first commercial license for a wave energy park in the United States," says Charles. "Remarkably, the permit is for thirty-five years, a strong statement about how the U.S. government views the long-term potential for wave energy."

When OPT is ready to deploy the Mark 3 PowerBuoy, they'll tow it two and a half miles off the coast of Reedsport, Oregon, connect it to a three-point mooring system, and ballast it to rise upright. The forty-foot-wide (12 meters) device, which looks a little like the Seattle Space Needle, will extend more than a hundred feet (30 meters) into the ocean and stick up thirty feet (9 meters) from the surface. If all goes well, as the PowerBuoy heaves up and down in the waves, it will generate up to 150 kilowatts of electricity, enough for more than a hundred homes.

When OPT gets the green light for grid connection, electricity from the PowerBuoy will travel through a cable on the sea floor to the local grid. From there the electricity will be sent out all over Reedsport, to power the lights in the Safeway grocery store, Highland Elementary School, and the Umpqua Lighthouse. It will fuel the fryers in Fitzpatrick's Crabby Café, the ovens in the Sugar Shack Bakery, and the freezer for the ice cream in Don's Diner. It will run dishwashers, computers, and televisions all across town. "This electricity will come from the ocean that the locals look at, fish in, swim in, surf in, and enjoy every single day," says Charles. "They will get this power without needing long transmission lines, without burning fossil fuels, without polluting."

Later, when OPT expands their wave park, an array of ten buoys could generate 1.5 megawatts of electricity, enough to power more than a thousand homes. "One of the nice things about our system is that you typically begin building a small power station," says George. "The customer will then say, 'This works very nicely.' It is a relatively easy thing to expand the wave power station; you simply add more buoys." The Reedsport deployment is only the first of a wave of projects that could energize our world. OPT is also developing projects in Australia, Japan, and Europe. Other developers have high hopes as well.

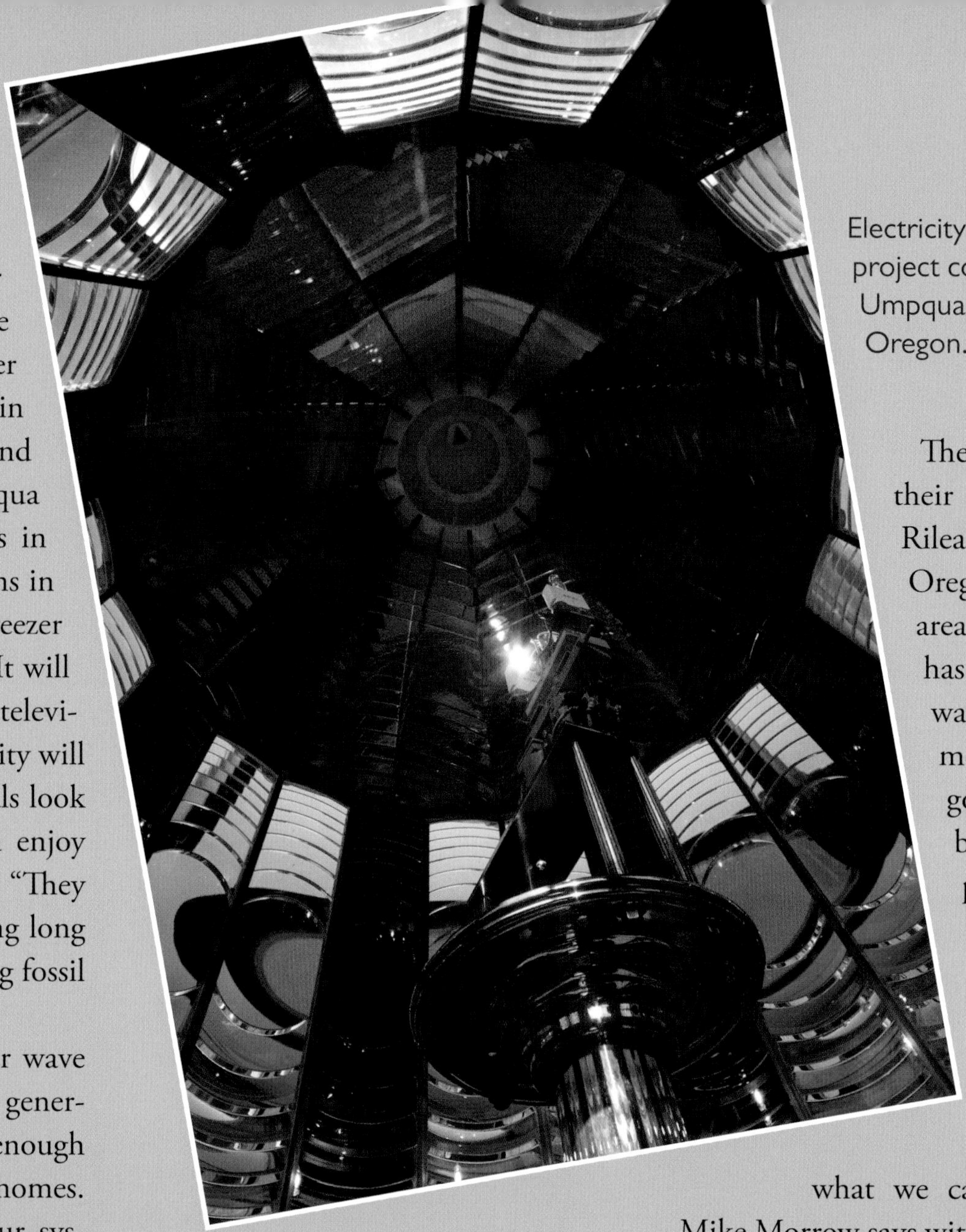

Electricity from OPT's wave energy project could power the bulbs of the Umpqua Lighthouse in Reedsport, Oregon.

The Mikes have set their sights on Camp Rilea in Warrenton, Oregon, where an area of shallow water has been cleared for wave energy development near the Oregon National Guard base. The guard has plans for the base to become net-zero in its energy usage, and the Mikes' DMP could help. "I can't wait to see what we can do out there," Mike Morrow says with a smile. "Though from shore, there won't be anything to see." Ultimately, the Mikes imagine multiple arrays of ten DMPs at various locations up and down the coast making potentially dozens of megawatts of electricity.

OPT's PowerBuoy project is slated to be located in the waters off the Umpqua Lighthouse to take advantage of the area's powerful waves.

Columbia Power Technologies hopes to roll out clusters of StingRAYs, powering many thousands of homes. "Our power potential is very, very good," says Ken. Add to that the work of developers across the globe, and even if not every project goes as planned, the electricity generated from waves could make a real difference. "Like any human enterprise, there may be setbacks," Charles from OPT says. "But we have to take our inspiration from the ocean—and just keep it coming."

The race to make electricity from waves is not a race with only one winner. Rather, it's a race against time and against our dangerous dependence on fossil fuels. Worldwide levels of carbon dioxide, the biggest contributor to global warming, have hit a horrifying milestone, reaching heights never before encountered by humans. The greenhouse gas has risen to four hundred parts per million, a level last reached millions of years ago, when the world was much hotter and seas were much higher. Even if we manage to control emissions from burning coal, oil, and gas, we will likely run out of these fossil fuels someday. That's why when *any* of these wave energy pioneers contribute clean, renewable electricity to our grid, we all win.

The wave energy pioneer Annette von Jouanne playing in the waves with her family at the beach in Waldport, Oregon. From left Naiya, age eleven, Sydney, age thirteen, Annette, her husband, Alex Yokochi, and her son, Luke, age four.

The ocean is vast and varied, so there's room for many solutions to succeed. Perhaps one device will work better in mild waves while another design takes advantage of monster waves. One invention may work well in a sandy area while another performs best in a rocky environment. Submerged inventions like the Mikes' DMP might be the perfect fit for a shallow, nearshore spot, while an array of bobbing buoys draws power farther offshore.

Maybe, just maybe, there's an invention, something no one has thought of yet, something no one has even imagined, that offers yet another amazing way to harness the astounding power of waves. The best idea might still be out there for you to imagine and build and test and improve to perfection. "One exciting aspect of being a part of this groundbreaking field is that there's still so much room for the creativity of the next generation to have a huge impact, to make a real positive difference," says Annette.

The future of clean energy—and of the world—may lie with you, future wave energy pioneers. "This is such hard work," Annette says. "But it's also a lot of fun, and so worth it."

This view of earth taken from space demonstrates that one of the solutions to global climate change is as far-reaching as the problem. Wave-making oceans cover more than 70 percent of the planet's surface.

## Wave Words

**Aft** The back of a boat

**Backwash** Water retreating from shore back to the ocean

**Ballast** Extra weight added to a floating object to stabilize it

**Barrel or tube** The hollow part of a breaking wave, formed when the crest spills over

**Bow** The front of a boat

**Breaking wave** When the crest of a wave spills forward

**Chop** Small, irregular waves with peaks created when wind pushes ripples together

**Crest** The highest part of a wave

**Face** The front of the wave, from crest to trough

**Fetch** The distance over which wind blows across water in the same direction, generating waves; the longer the fetch, the bigger the waves

**Kilowatt** A measure of electrical power equivalent to 1,000 watts

**Lull** The calm period between sets of waves where waves are small or absent

**Megawatt** A measure of electrical power equivalent to 1,000 kilowatts, or 1,000,000 watts

**Port** The left side of a boat when facing forward

**Rogue waves** Massive waves formed when individual waves combine

**Set** A group of larger waves separated by lulls

**Shorebreak** An area of shallow water on the coast where waves break frequently

**Starboard** The right side of a boat when facing forward

**Swell** Waves that do not break; also, a cluster of waves

**Trough** The lowest part of a wave

**Tsunami** Large wave formed by displacement of land from an earthquake, volcanic eruption, or landslide

**Watt** A measure of electrical power used or generated

**Wave amplitude** The vertical distance from calm sea level to the crest of a wave; usually an average over a period of time

**Wave frequency** Number of wave crests passing a fixed point in a set amount of time

**Wave height** The vertical distance from the trough of a wave to its crest

**Wavelength** The distance between two consecutive crests (or two troughs)

**Wave period** The time it takes for two consecutive crests to pass a point


## A Big Wave of Thanks

I want to thank all the ocean energy professionals who so generously shared their thoughts and experiences with me in countless hours of interviews and site visits. This book would not have been possible without your help: Kevin Banister, Sean Barrett, Roger Bedard, George Boehlert, Dan Cox, Mike Delos-Reyes, Charles Dunleavy, Erik Friis-Madsen, Dexter Gauntlett, Howard Hanson, Erik Hammagren, Jason Killian, Justin Klure, Pukha Lenee-Bluhm, Terry Lettenmeier, Tim Maddux, Michael C. Miller, Debbie Montagna, Mike Morrow, Sean O'Neill, Joe Prudell, Fiona Reed, Ken Rhinefrank, Al Schacher, Deborah Smith, Linda Stitt, Luis Vega, and Alla Weinstein. I would like to offer special thanks to Annette von Jouanne, who has been graciously answering questions, providing updates, and allowing me to tag along as she worked ever since I first became interested in wave energy in 2006. You were the first inspiration for this book and I hope your work, and the work of your colleagues, will be an inspiration to the next generation of wave energy pioneers.

I would also like to offer my deep appreciation to Erin Dees, Tatty Bartholomew, and Meredith Meier for their stellar research, editing, and transcribing skills; to the writers Addie Boswell, Nancy Coffelt, Melissa Dalton, Ruth Feldman, Ellen Howard, Barbara Kerley, Amber Keyser, Sabina Rascol, Nicole Schreiber, and Emily Whitman for their insightful comments and suggestions; and to photographers Jeff Basinger and Erin Fitzpatrick-Bjorn for their good work and good humor.

Thank you to Laura Helmuth for your early interest in wave energy and in my writing. And finally, a big thanks to Cynthia Platt, Christine Krones, Lisa DiSarro, Rachel Wasdyke, and the whole Houghton Mifflin Harcourt team for all your wonderful support and guidance.


## Notes

CHAPTER ONE: *The Power of Waves*

A wave that is just a foot and a half . . . : Casey, *The Wave*, 7.

Shipwreck data: Casey, *The Wave* ; Rosenthal, "Results of the MAXWAVE Project."

*Caledonian Star* incident: Smith, *Extreme Waves,* 184–85; quotations from BBC, *Freak Waves.*

. . . provide more than 80 percent of our nation's energy demands: U.S. Energy Information Administration, *Monthly Energy Review.* Fossil fuel total reported at 82 percent.

Global warming data: climate.nasa.gov, Key Indicators, Evidence, Causes, Effects, and Consensus.

Wave energy could provide as much as a *third* of the nation's electricity: Electric Power Research Institute, *Mapping and Assessment.* This study puts the total recoverable wave energy potential off the coast of the United States alone at 1,170 terawatts, almost one-third of the 4,000 terawatts of electricity used in the country each year.

That's the equivalent of the energy in more than 93 billion gallons of oil: U.S. Energy Information Administration, "How Much Coal." The U.S. Energy Information Administration estimates that 0.08 gallon of oil is the equivalent of 1 kilowatt of electricity. The number of gallons of oil needed to generate 1 terawatt would be 0.08 times 1 billion, or 80,000,000. Multiplied by 1,170 terawatts, that equals 93,600,000,000 gallons.

. . . more than twice the power produced by all U.S. hydroelectric dams, solar power, and wind power projects combined: In *Electric Power Monthly* (March 2013), the U.S. Energy Information Administration reports that U.S. power plants using renewable energy sources generated about 12 percent of our electricity in 2012. One-third is more than 24 percent.

. . . and enough to power *every home* in the nation: U.S. Energy Information Administration's *Annual Energy Review 2011* reports that 22 percent of electricity use in the United States was residential. One-third is more than 22 percent.

"To be successful . . .": Justin Klure, interview with author, 2013.

Power Near the People: Data is from United Nations Atlas of the Oceans, "Human Settlements on the Coast." The map was created from two maps: Population density is from Encyclopedia Britannica, *World Atlas*, 24–25; average annual wave power from a map created with WorldWaves software using data from European Centre for Medium-Range Weather Forecasts by senior ocean wave climatologists Stephen Barstow and Gunnar Mork of Fugro Oceanor, Trondheim, Norway, March 2008.

### CHAPTER TWO: *The Mikes*

All information and quotations from author interviews and emails with Mike Morrow and Mike Delos-Reyes, 2012 and 2013, and site visit 2013.

### CHAPTER THREE: *Building Buoys*

All information and quotations from author interviews and emails with Dan Cox, 2008, and Annette von Jouanne, 2007, 2008, 2012, and 2013. Adapted from Rusch, "Catching a Wave," with additional reporting and fact-checking.

Annette von Jouanne also credits her late colleague Alan Wallace, who passed away in 2006, with helping to develop the wave energy research program in the energy systems group at Oregon State University.

Working with Watts: Wattages graphic is from U.S. Energy Information Administration, *Residential Energy Consumption Survey,* 2009 (the most recent year data was available).

### CHAPTER FOUR: *Steel in the Water*

All information and quotations on SeaBeav1 from author interviews and emails with Annette von Jouanne, 2007, 2008, 2012, and 2013, except the following:

Storm data: Tomlinson, "Offshore Storm"; Wilson, "Wind Gusts Offer a Preview."

"Weather Sinks Wave Buoy Test for Season": Odegard, "Weather Sinks."

All information and quotations on AquaBuOY from 2013 author interviews and emails with Alla Weinstein, former CEO of AquaEnergy and former general manager of the ocean renewables technology group for Finavera Renewables except the following:

"The race right now . . . ": Tobias, "Canadian Firm to Test.

"It performed exactly . . . ": Dillman, "Sunken Buoy Rescue Under Way."

"It was a prototype . . . ": Ross, "Wave Energy Buoy Plunges."

"I know there may be concerns . . . ": "Wave Energy Buoy Sinks."

"The fishing community was . . . ": Annette von Jouanne, interview with author.

"We couldn't let . . . ": Annette von Jouanne, interview with author.

Wild Wave Inventions of the World: All information comes from the companies' websites and from spokespeople, including Linsey Morrice; www.aquamarinepower.com; www.oceanlinx.com; www.pelamiswave.com; Erik Friis-Madsen; www.wavedragon.net; and www.tecdragon.pt.

### CHAPTER FIVE: *Ducking the Waves*

All information and quotations from author interviews and emails with Mike Morrow and Mike Delos-Reyes, 2012 and 2013, and site visit 2013.

Saving Sea Creatures: George Boehlert, interview with author, 2008; "Impacts on the Environment," NNMREC website, nnmrec.oregonstate.edu/impacts-environment; Annette von Jouanne, interviews with author, 2007 and 2008; and Elizabeth Rusch, "Catching a Wave," *Smithsonian,* July 2009.

### CHAPTER SIX: *Testing, Testing*

All information and quotations from author interviews and emails with Annette von Jouanne and Justin Klure, 2012 and 2013, and observations from site visit by boat to the test berth August 2012, except the following:

"Twenty-foot swells . . .": Danko, "NZ Wave Power Device"; and emails with Justin Klure.

Annette von Jouanne and her colleagues developed the Ocean Sentinel with AXYS Technologies. Her team included Sean Moran, Ean Amon, and Terry Lettenmaier.

The WET-NZ wave energy converter is the product of a research consortium between Callaghan Innovation, a New Zealand Crown Entity, and Power Projects Limited (PPL), a Wellington, New Zealand, private company. The Oregon deployment was managed by Northwest Energy Innovations (NWEI), a Portland, Oregon, firm.

Oregon State University's NNMREC team included Belinda Batten (director), Sean Moran (ocean test facilities manager), Annette von Jouanne, Bob Paasch, Ted Brekken, Ean Amon, Alex Yokochi, Solomon Yim, Tuba Ozkan-Haller, Mick Haller, Kaety Hildenbrand (Oregon Sea Grant, liaison with fishing community/FINE), and Flaxen Conway.

### CHAPTER SEVEN: *Big Power from Big Seas*

All information and quotations from author interviews and emails with Ken Rhinefrank, Joe Prudell, and Al Schacher, 2012 and 2013, and observations from site visits to O. H. Hinsdale Wave Research Laboratory, November 2012.

### CHAPTER EIGHT: *Saved by Waves?*

"You get the feeling . . . ": Yang, "Buoy System Harnesses Wave Energy."

"A big part of our story . . . " to "The electricity will come from the ocean . . . ": Charles Dunleavy, interview with author, 2013.

"One of the nice things . . . ": *Wall Street Transcript.*

"I can't wait to see . . . ": Mike Morrow, interview with author, 2013.

"Our power potential . . . ": Ken Rhinefrank, interview with author, 2012.

"Like any human enterprise . . . ": Charles Dunleavy, interview with author, 2013.

Greenhouse gas milestone: National Oceanic and Atmospheric Administration, "Carbon Dioxide at NOAA's Mauna Loa Observatory."

"One exciting aspect . . . " and "This is such hard work . . . ": Annette von Jouanne, interview with author, 2013.

## Sources

Banister, Kevin (former vice president for business development for Finavera Renewables). Interview with author, 2013.

Barstow, Stephen (senior ocean wave climatologist, Fugro Oceanor, Trondheim, Norway). Emails with author, 2013 .

BBC, *Freak Waves,* documentary, aired November 14, 2002.

Boehlert, George (marine scientist and director of Hatfield Marine Science Center, Newport, Oregon). Interview with author, 2008.

Casey, Susan. *The Wave: In Pursuit of the Rogues, Freaks and Giants of the Ocean*. New York: Doubleday, 2010.

Cox, Daniel (former director of O. H. Hinsdale Wave Research Laboratory, Oregon State University). Interview with author, 2008.

Danko, Peter. "NZ Wave Power Device Heading to Hawaii After Oregon Test." EarthTechling, September 30, 2012. www.earthtechling.com.

Delos-Reyes, Mike (chief scientist, M3 Wave Energy Systems, Salem, Oregon). Interviews with author, 2013.

Dillman, Terry. "Sunken Buoy Rescue Under Way." *Newport News Times,* July 25, 2008.

Dunleavy, Charles (chief executive officer, Ocean Power Technologies, Pennington, New Jersey). Interview with author, 2013.

Electric Power Research Institute, *Mapping and Assessment of the United States Wave Energy Resource* (Electric Power Research Institute: Palo Alto, Calif., December 2011).

Encyclopedia Britannica, *World Atlas,* Chicago: Encyclopedia Brittanica, Inc., 2011.

Gauntlett, Dexter (research analyst for Navigant Research's Smart Energy program). Interviews with author, 2012 and 2013.

Hammagren, Erik (R&D engineer—mechanical, Columbia Power Technologies, Corvallis, Oregon). Interviews and site visit with author, 2012 and 2013.

Killian, Jason (faculty research assistant, O. H. Hinsdale Wave Research Laboratory, Corvallis, Oregon). Interviews and site visit with author, 2012 and 2013.

Klure, Justin (managing partner, Pacific Energy Ventures, and consultant with Northwest Energy Innovations on the WET-NZ deployment, Portland, Oregon). Interviews with author, 2013.

Lenee-Bluhm, Pukha (senior R&D engineer—data analysis, Columbia Power Technologies, Corvallis, Oregon). Interviews and site visits with author, 2012 and 2013.

Lettenmeier, Terry (Ph.D. engineering candidate, Oregon State University, Corvallis, Oregon). Interview with author and site visit, 2012.

Maddux, Tim (faculty research associate, O. H. Hinsdale Wave Research Laboratory, Corvallis, Oregon). Interviews and site visit with author, 2012 and 2013.

Montagna, Deborah (vice president of business and product development, Ocean Power Technologies, Pennington, New Jersey). Phone conversations and emails with author, 2012 and 2013.

Morrow, Mike (chief technical officer, M3 Wave Energy Systems, Salem, Oregon). Interviews and site visit with author, 2013.

National Aeronautics and Space Administration. climate.nasa.gov, Key Indicators, Evidence, Causes, Effects, and Consensus sections.

National Oceanic and Atmospheric Administration, "Carbon Dioxide at NOAA's Mauna Loa Observatory Reaches New Milestone: Tops 400 ppm." NOAA press release, May 10, 2013.

Northwest National Marine Renewable Energy Center, "Impacts on the Environment," NNMREC website, nnmrec.oregonstate.edu/impacts-environment.

Nouquere, Pierre T., ed., *Perfect Waves: The Endless Allure of the Ocean*. New York: Abrams, 2006.

Odegard, Kyle. "Weather Sinks Wave Buoy Test for Season." *Corvallis Gazette-Times,* October 19, 2007.

Parker, Bruce. *The Power of the Sea*. New York: Palgrave Macmillan, 2010.

Prudell, Joseph H. (senior R&D engineer—electrical, Columbia Power Technologies, Corvallis, Oregon). Interviews and site visits with author, 2012 and 2013.

Rhinefrank, Ken (vice president of research, Columbia Power Technologies, Corvallis, Oregon). Interviews and site visits with author, 2012 and 2013.

Rosenthal, W., "Results of the MAXWAVE Project," Institute of Coastal Research, Geesthacht, Germany.

Ross, Winston. "Professor Hopes to Catch Wave of the Future." *Eugene Register-Guard,* July 9, 2007.

——. "Wave Energy Buoy Plunges to Ocean Floor." *Eugene Register-Guard*, November 1, 2007.

Rusch, Elizabeth. "Catching a Wave." *Smithsonian,* July 2009.

Schacher, Alphonse (senior R&D engineer—controls, Columbia Power Technologies, Corvallis, Oregon). Interviews and site visits with author, 2012 and 2013.

Smith, Craig B. *Extreme Waves*. Washington, D.C.: Joseph Henry Press, 2006.

Stitt, Linda (executive assistant, Ocean Power Technologies, Pennington, New Jersey). Emails with author, 2012 and 2013.

Tobias, Lori. "Canadian Firm to Test Wave Energy Buoy." *Oregonian,* September 1, 2007.

——. "Wave Energy Buoy Sinks Day Before Its Removal." *Oregonian,* November 1, 2007.

Tomlinson, Stuart. "Offshore Storm Not Expected to Cause Wind Damage Inland." *Oregonian,* October 9, 2007.

United Nations Atlas of the Oceans. "Human Settlements on the Coast." www.oceanatlas.com

U.S. Department of Energy.

U.S. Energy Information Administration. *Annual Energy Review 2011*. www.eia.gov/total-energy/data/annual/[df/aer.pdf——. *Electric Power Monthly,* Table 1.2, March 2013.

——. *Monthly Energy Review,* May 2012.

——. *Residential Energy Consumption Survey,* 2009. www.eia.gov/consumption/residential

——. " How Much Coal, Natural Gas, or Petroleum Is Used to Generate a Kilowatt-Hour of Electricity?" Frequently Asked Questions.www.eia.gov/tools/faqs/faq.cfm?id=667&t=6.

von Jouanne, Annette (professor of electrical and computer engineering, Oregon State University). Interviews and site visits with author, 2007, 2008, 2012, and 2013.

*Wall Street Transcript*. "George W. Taylor" (CEO interview). TWST.com, November 5, 2007.

Weinstein, Alla (former CEO of AquaEnergy and former general manager of the ocean renewables technology group for Finavera Renewables). Interview with author, 2013.

Wilson, Kimberly. "Wind Gusts Offer a Preview of Stormy Days." *Oregonian,* October 19, 2007.

Yang, John. "Buoy System Harnesses Wave Energy." ABCNews.go.com, June 29, 2011, abcnews.go.com/Technology/CuttingEdge/story?id=98434&page=1#.UctQpOBj5Hg.

## Read—and Surf—More

TWO BASIC BOOKS ABOUT WAVES

Berger, Melvin, and Gilda Berger. *What Makes an Ocean Wave? Questions and Answers About Oceans and Ocean Life*. New York: Scholastic, 2000.

Kampion, Drew. *Waves: From Surfing to Tsunami*. Gibbs Smith: Salt Lake City, 2005.

NATIONAL OCEAN ENERGY CENTERS

Three national centers support ocean energy development and each has a website full of fascinating information. Learn more about Annette's center, the Northwest National Marine Renewable Energy Center, at nnmrec.oregonstate.edu.

The Hawai'i National Marine Renewable Energy Center (HINMREC) at the University of Hawai'i supports developers of wave-energy devices as well as devices that take advantage of the temperature differences found at different depths of the ocean (known as ocean thermal energy conversion): hinmrec.hnei.hawaii.edu.

The Southeast National Marine Renewable Energy Center (SNMREC) at Florida Atlantic University supports development and testing of devices that harness the power of ocean currents as well as temperature differences at different depths of the ocean.

WAVE-ENERGY WEBSITES

Columbia Power Technologies: www.columbiapwr.com

M3 Wave Energy Systems: www.m3wave.com

O. H. Hinsdale Wave Research Laboratory: wave.oregonstate.edu

OSU's Wallace Energy Systems and Renewables Facility: eecs.engr.oregonstate.edu/wesrf

WET-NZ: www.wavenergy.co.nz; www.nwenergyinnovations.com

OTHER RELEVANT WEBSITES

NASA's Climate Kids website: www.climatekids.nasa.gov

Oregon Wave Energy Trust: www.owet.org

U.S. Bureau of Ocean Energy Management: www.boem.gov

U.S. Department of Energy: www.energy.gov

U.S. Energy Information Administration's Energy Kids website: www.eia.gov/kids/

**RECENT UPDATE: As this book went to press, OPT began shifting focus to a commercial wave energy project off the coast of Australia, and the Mikes got the green light to temporarily deploy a scale model DMP near Camp Rilea off the coast of Warrenton, Oregon.**

## Index

Page numbers in **bold** type refer to photos.

Amon, Ean, **55**
AquaBuOY energy device, **33**, 33–37, **36**, **37**
Aquamarine Power's Oyster 800 energy device, 35, **35**

BlueRAY energy device, 56
Brekken, Ted, **55**
Brown, Adam, **55**
Burns, Joe, 66

Clark, Myke, 36, 37
Columbia Power Technologies
  BlueRAY energy device, 56
  future plans, 72
  SeaRAY energy device, **56**, 56–57
  StingRAY energy device, 57–63, **58**, **59**, **60**, 72

Delos-Reyes, Mike
  childhood building projects, 14, 14
  college wave-energy project, 16–21, 17, 18, 20, 21
  construction and testing of DMP energy device, 42–45, **43**, **44**, **45**
  construction of wave flume, 41, 41
  feasibility considerations for wave-energy device, 39–41
  future plans, 70
DMP (Delos-Reyes Morrow Pressure Device)
  design and construction of scale model, **42**, 42–43, **43**
  development grants, 42
  future development plans, 70
  pros and cons of underwater design, **39**, 39–41
  testing at Hinsdale Large Wave Flume, 43–45, **44**, **45**
Dunleavy, Charles, 66–69, 72

electricity
  harnessing of wave energy for, 10
  household usage, 28
  loss during transport over long distances, 11
  power grids, 53
  *See also* wave energy
energy. *See* wave energy
energy devices. *See* wave-energy devices
environmental concerns
  global warming, 10, 72
  impact of wave-energy devices, 37, **39**, 40, **40**, 52, **52**

Finavera Renewables (AquaBuOY), **33**, 33–37, **36**, **37**
FINE (Fishermen Involved in Natural Energy), **50**, 50–52, **52**

global warming, 10, 72

Hammagren, Erik, **58**, **59**, **61**, **62**
Hinsdale lab
  Large Wave Flume, 19, **19**, 28, **29**, **44**
  Tsunami Basin, **54**, 57, **57**, **58**
Hudspeth, Robert, 17

Klure, Justin, 10, 50, 53

Lettenmeier, Terry, 47, 51–53

Maddux, Tim, 58–59, 62

marine animals and environment, 37, **39**, 40, **40**, 52, **52**

Mikes, the. *See* Delos-Reyes, Mike; Morrow, Mike

Miller, Mike, 41

Morrow, Mike

- childhood engineering projects and observations, **13**, 13–16, **14**, **16**
- college wave-energy project, 16–21, **17**, **18**, **20**, **21**
- construction and testing of DMP energy device, **42**, 42–45, **44**, **45**
- construction of wave flume, 41
- feasibility considerations for wave-energy device, **38**, 39–41
- future plans, 70

M3 Wave Energy Systems. See Delos-Reyes, Mike; Morrow, Mike

Northwest National Marine Renewable Energy Center (NNMREC), 48, **48**

O. H. Hinsdale Wave Research Laboratory

- Large Wave Flume, 19, **19**, 28, **29**, **44**
- Tsunami Basin, **54**, 57, **57**, **58**

ocean energy. *See* wave energy

Oceanlinx's energy devices, 35, **35**

Ocean Power Technologies (OPT)

- commercial license for wave energy park, 65, 68
- future customers in Reedsport, Oregon, 70, **70**
- future projects, 70
- PowerBuoy energy device, **66**, 66–70, **67**, **68**, **69**, **71**
- work with investors, 66

Ocean Sentinel ocean test berth, **47**, 47–49, 52–53, **53**

OPT. *See* Ocean Power Technologies (OPT)

Oregon State University

- Northwest National Marine Renewable Energy Center (NNMREC) partnership, 48
- O. H. Hinsdale Large Wave Flume, 19, **19**, 28, **29**, **44**
- O. H. Hinsdale Tsunami Basin, **54**, 57, **57**, **58**
- Weatherford Hall, **12**
- WESRF power lab, **55**

Pavlik, Chuck, **50**, 50–52, **52**

Pelamis Wave Machine energy device, 34, **34**

Persson, Göran, 8–9

PowerBuoy energy device, **66**, 66–70, **67**, **68**, **69**, **71**

Prudell, Joe, **55**, 55–62, **58**, **59**, **60**

renewable energy, 10, 72

Rhinefrank, Ken, **55**, 55–63, **61**, **62**, 72

Schacher, Al, **55**, 55–61, **62**

SeaBeav1 energy device, **31**, 31–33, **32**

SeaRAY energy device, **56**, 56–57

Stillinger, Chad, **55**

StingRAY energy device, 57–63, **58**, **59**, **60**, 72

Taylor, George W., **65**, 65–66, 70

TRIAXYS data collection buoy, 51, **51**

University of Washington, 48

von Jouanne, Annette

- assistant professorship at Oregon State University, **22**, 23, 24
- on bad publicity affecting funding and research, 33, 37
- childhood engineering projects and career aspirations, 23–24
- concern for environment and animals, 24, 40
- family, **23**, **26**, **72**
- linear generator prototype and testing, 25–29, **26**, **27**, **29**
- on potential for creativity in wave-energy field, 72
- power lab team, **55**
- SeaBeav1 energy device design and testing, **31**, 31–33, 32
- support for wave-energy developers, 47–48, 50–53
- swimming and surfing, **23**, **24**, 24–25, **26**

Wave Dragon energy device, 34, **34**

wave energy

- designated development area in Oregon, 70
- earth's wave-making potential, **73**
- first commercial license for wave energy park, 65, 68
- proximity of oceans to populated areas, 11, **11**
- as renewable alternative to fossil fuels, 10, 72
- resources for more information, 78
- vocabulary words, 74

wave-energy devices

- AquaBuOY, **33**, 33–37, **36**, **37**
- BlueRAY, 56
- challenges posed by ocean environment, 10, 41, 67
- designs currently under development, 34–35, **34–35**
- DMP (Delos-Reyes Morrow Pressure Device), 39–45, **42**, **43**, **44**, **45**, 70
- impact on marine animals and environment, 37, **39**, 40, **40**, 52, **52**
- linear generator design, 25–29, **26**, **27**
- low-budget college project, 16–21, **17**, **18**, **20**, **21**
- movements in response to waves, 25, **25**
- PowerBuoy, **66**, 66–70, **67**, **68**, **69**, **71**
- SeaBeav1, **31**, 31–33, **32**
- SeaRAY, **56**, 56–57
- StingRAY, 57–63, **58**, **59**, **60**, 72
- three-point mooring systems, 58
- variety of design possibilities, 72
- wattage ratings, 28
- WET-NZ (Wave Energy Technology—New Zealand), **49**, 49–53, **53**

wave-energy device testing facilities

- Northwest National Marine Renewable Energy Center (NNMREC), 48
- O. H. Hinsdale Large Wave Flume, 19, **19**, 28, **29**, **44**
- O. H. Hinsdale Tsunami Basin, 54, 57, **57**, **58**
- Ocean Sentinel ocean test berth, **47**, 47–49, 52–53, **53**
- testing launch site, **46**

waves

- collection of data on, 51, **51**
- fifty-year storm conditions, 60
- formation and parts of, 15, **15**
- power of, **6**, 7, **30**
- ships' encounters with, **8**, 8–10, **9**
- surfing, **11**
- underwater pressure changes, 14–16

Weinstein, Alla, 36, 37

WET-NZ (Wave Energy Technology—New Zealand) energy device, **49**, 49–53, **53**

# SCIENTISTS IN THE FIELD

## Where Science Meets Adventure

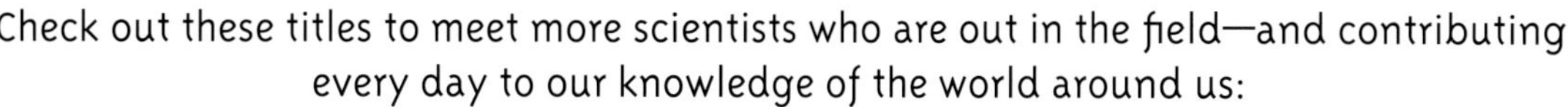

Check out these titles to meet more scientists who are out in the field—and contributing every day to our knowledge of the world around us:

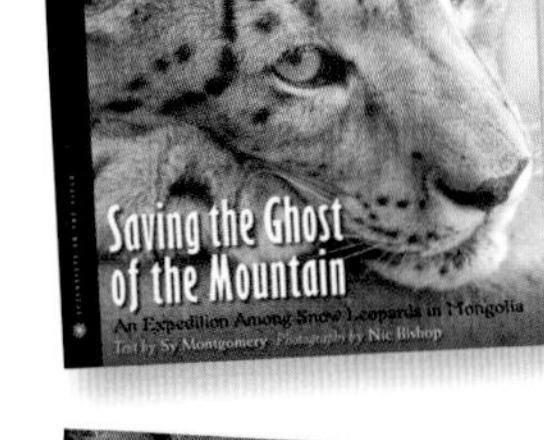

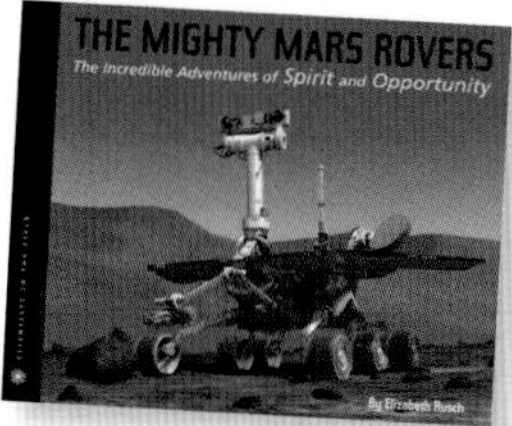

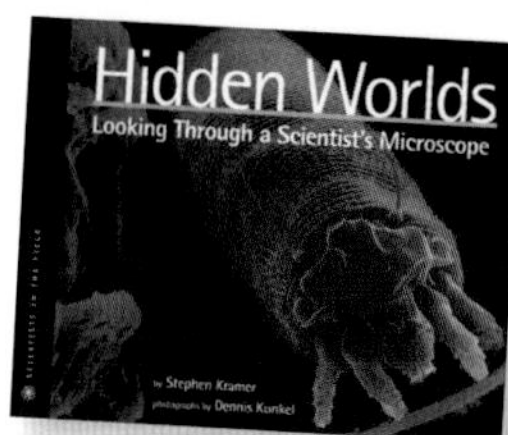

Looking for even more adventure? Craving updates on the work of your favorite scientists, as well as in-depth video footage, audio, photography, and more? Then visit the new Scientists in the Field website!

www.sciencemeetsadventure.com